Slow Love

Slow Love

How I Lost My Job,
Put on My Pajamas,
and Found Happiness

Dominique Browning

A PLUME BOOK

PLUME
Published by the Penguin Group

Penguin Group (USA) Inc., 375 Hudson Street, New York, New York 10014, U.S.A. • Penguin Group (Canada), 90 Eglinton Avenue East, Suite 700, Toronto, Ontario, Canada M4P 2Y3 (a division of Pearson Penguin Canada Inc.) • Penguin Books Ltd., 80 Strand, London WC2R 0RL, England • Penguin Ireland, 25 St. Stephen's Green, Dublin 2, Ireland (a division of Penguin Books Ltd.) • Penguin Group (Australia), 250 Camberwell Road, Camberwell, Victoria 3124, Australia (a division of Pearson Australia Group Pty. Ltd.) • Penguin Books India Pvt. Ltd., 11 Community Centre, Panchsheel Park, New Delhi – 110 017, India • Penguin Group (NZ), 67 Apollo Drive, Rosedale, Auckland 0632, New Zealand (a division of Pearson New Zealand Ltd.) • Penguin Books (South Africa) (Pty.) Ltd., 24 Sturdee Avenue, Rosebank, Johannesburg 2196, South Africa

Penguin Books Ltd., Registered Offices: 80 Strand, London WC2R 0RL, England

Published by Plume, a member of Penguin Group (USA) Inc. Previously published by Atlas & Co.

First Plume Printing, September 2011

10   9   8   7   6   5   4   3   2   1

Ⓟ REGISTERED TRADEMARK—MARCA REGISTRADA

CIP data is available.
ISBN 978-0-452-29750-0 (pbk.)

Printed in the United States of America

Penguin is committed to publishing works of quality and integrity.
In that spirit, we are proud to offer this book to our readers;
however, the story, the experiences, and the words
are the author's alone.

For
Amanda Urban,
who changed my life,
and
Patricia Yarberry Allen,
who saved it

CONTENTS

SLOW LOVE

The gloom of the world is but a shadow;
behind it, yet within our reach, is joy.
Take joy.

—FRA GIOVANNI GIOCONDO

PROLOGUE

M Y EIGHTY-YEAR-OLD French cousin's voice rings in my ears. We are in Paris; I have squeezed in time to see her during a hectic business trip. We are walking down the Champs Élysées, which to her eye looks the same as it did in the late '30s, when she arrived here from Casablanca. She survived World War II by claiming to be a Catholic; she lost much of her family in Auschwitz. Now she is learning to live without her husband of fifty years. He was twenty years her senior, so it hasn't upset the natural order of things for him to go first; in the last ten years he was miserable with illness. "An older man," she used to tell me when I was in my twenties, living with her, "an older man is a wonderful thing for a young girl. He knows how to hold her in his arms. He knows how to make love to a woman. He knows how to waltz. But never marry an older man, chérie. I was young. I wanted to wear my dancing slippers for years. Before long, all he wanted from me were his bedroom slippers."

Colette is an elegant person, perfectly groomed in a classic style of dress. She has always been a gracious hostess, a busy mother, and an ardent shopper. But today, it isn't her husband who is on her mind. We are strolling slowly, her arm in the crook of mine. She is, as usual, immaculately turned out; her bag matches her shoes, her coat is a pearly white wool. Today, she wants to talk about drugs.

"*Le Prozac!*" she begins shouting, to my disbelief. She has stopped in the middle of the sidewalk, her arms spread as if to embrace the world. "*Le Prozac! C'est un miracle!*" I turn and stare at her, and she sweeps her hands dramatically down her coat. "*Le Prozac! C'est un imperméable*—a raincoat! Everything just washes off. The rain comes down—poof! Gone. Nothing bothers me anymore. Why didn't I find this miracle thirty years ago?" She fixes me with a penetrating look. I am her age, thirty years ago. "Finally, I can slow down. No more worries. I can have peace. *J'adore le Prozac!*"

So there you have it, I'm thinking, eighty years and finally she's found a way to quiet what must have been a constant anxiety in her head—an incessant voice urging perfection, order, restraint, and speed in all things: do more, do it better, do it faster, faster, faster. Now here she is, at eighty, almost weeping with relief and joy at letting go of that clamor.

But do I listen to her? Do I really hear what she is saying? Of course not.

I return to New York and leap right back into my frenetic life. Nothing moves fast enough. Everything is great! Everything is insane! Work is driving me crazy? I love my job! My relationships with men go nowhere? So what! I don't see enough of my friends? Later! There isn't enough time to do all the things I want to do? I don't even know what I want to do! I seem to spend all my time doing all the things everyone else wants me to do? But that's fine, really! Who has time to think about this stuff, anyway? That's life, isn't it?

Until suddenly one day it isn't.

Until suddenly I've lost my job. I've lost the very thing that defined my days, paced and regulated my life. The wind is knocked out of me. Suddenly I'm floundering. I'm terrified. And I'm not alone. All around me, for all sorts of different reasons, by 2008 thousands of people are being knocked off course, losing their bearings. We're losing our jobs, ending careers, losing life savings, losing homes. Like everyone else, I'm scrambling to pick myself up. Mine is not a story of financial ruin, though certainly I have had to alter the contours of my life without a regular salary. It is a story of psychological collapse, of struggling to start over again—and not make all the same mistakes.

No, scratch that. That's a bad habit I am determined to shed, the habit of casting doubt over every decision I've ever made—going as far back as high school!—that's led to where I am now. I suspect that no matter what other choices I might have made, I still would have been running, running, running for all I was worth, because I didn't know any better. Most of us don't. And all that racing around wasn't all bad, either. It simply wasn't . . . sustainable. Or fulfilling.

So now I'm faced with two possible responses. Either I crack up, or I use this trauma as an opportunity to grow.

Of course I crack up. I become infantile, in my way. Just enough to start learning how to live all over again. Just enough to learn to turn to friends and ask for help. Just enough to realize that it is time to redefine what success means to me. What follows, then, is an account of my journey through a painful time. My story is particular to me, mine alone, as are my family, my friends, my responses, my habits, and my heartbreaks. But the lessons I have learned are born of emotions that are universal.

At the start of this journey, all I could think about was loss: lost work; my children who had left home; my house slipping from my grasp; my parents slipping into their last years. Lost love, on top of it all, because I was finally forced to confront the failure of a relationship that had preoccupied me for seven years. Attachment, abandonment, misery—I was plagued, until, mysteriously, something in my brain shifted into a new gear, and I was no longer experiencing all the changes I was going through as the loss of everything I loved. Instead, I began feeling the value of change and . . . experience, events—yes, some of them calamitous—that have unexpectedly come to enhance the quality of my days.

In other words, life.

It never gets easier. But if we're paying attention, it can get simpler.

Le Prozac, miracle though it might be, doesn't turn out to be my answer. I've never been one to let things wash off me. If anything, I feel more deeply than ever. The pace of my life has slowed down, even as the pace of the world seems to have quickened. As it turns out—and I didn't know it would when I began writing—this is ultimately a book about what comes of slow living: slow love.

Now, slow food is a concept I could embrace the minute I first heard about it. I thought all I had to do was let other people do the slow thing, so that I could enjoy a fabulous meal. By contrast, slow living—slowing *myself* down—as an operative concept, was alien to me. I never would have done it if I hadn't been forced to. But as I began to appreciate what was happening in my life, I realized that slow living set a gentle, healing pace. It allowed me to catch my breath, to rethink, no, to reexperience and "re-feel" my priorities. It showed me a way to settle in for the long haul, what's left of it.

Slow living, I have come to understand, opens up the prospect of slow love, the most sustaining sort of love I have ever known—a love that comes of an unhurried and focused attention to the simplest things, available to all of us, at any time, should we choose to engage: family, friendship, food, music, art, books, our bodies, our minds, our souls, and the life that blooms and buzzes all around us. Perhaps even more importantly, slow love comes out of the quiet hours, out of learning from the silence that is always there when we want it. I still hardly know how to describe it, but somehow, during the long months after getting knocked off my career track, and at the same time having to face the end of an intense love affair, I connected with something under and beneath and over everything, and caught a glimmer of peace. I still have my moody seasons, the occasional blights, the drooping days, yet even then I feel as if I have grown a new taproot, one that reaches deeper into nourishing soil. I am more resilient. If I had to pin it down, I would say I finally fell open to the miracle of this world.

Slow love is about knowing what you've got *before* it's gone.

I've spent hours, lately, from dawn to dark, planting a new garden. I've been obsessed with it, without really questioning it, just giving in to the need and to the weird, mindless, mindful therapy—hands in the heavy, clay earth, shovel clanging against stone, pain vibrating into my neck and back, not knowing what time it is until darkness has fallen and I can no longer see what I am doing. As I thunk my tiny plants out of their plastic pots, I feel amazement and wonder at the fragile, slender white roots that are all that connect those plants to any hope of life. Looking at those roots, I keep thinking, Is that it? Is it possible? Is that all you have to keep you going? It is hard to believe that out of those pale, tentative threads will come color, and shape, and fragrance, and height. I put those plants into the ground with hope, and with the understanding that that's all I can do. Give them a start. It seems like . . . not much.

But, as a friend of mine put it, when I pointed to the one scrawny snowdrop that had made it through the winter in my new garden and told him how much I missed the carpet of white flowers that used to appear every spring at the front door of my old house—"So? Now you've got only one snowdrop. Concentrate on that one. Look at it like you've never seen a snowdrop before. See what happens."

I welcome you into my story with the image of me on my hands and knees on the cool, damp earth, peering into the heart of a flower, hoping none of the neighbors see me and think I'm stoned or I've lost my mind.

And it is amazing.

One snowdrop can give you more than a thousand—if you let it.

That is slow love.

The Fall

Ridiculous the waste sad time
Stretching before and after
— T. S. ELIOT, "Four Quartets"

1. SATURDAY

F OR NEARLY THIRTEEN years, I had a job as the editor of
House & Garden, a magazine that celebrated the good life. It
would be an understatement to describe this enterprise as part of
a company that was decidedly *not* in the business of philosophical, spiritual, or moral soul-searching. Condé Nast's roots and
branches are in the material world. So, though we maintained
high standards in writing and photography, and included stories in the magazine about spirituality, sustainability, and social
responsibility wherever we could (and worried about offending
gas-guzzling car advertisers), the good life in *House & Garden*
generally meant cultivating your own backyard rather than being involved in the body politic. As much as we pushed against
the limits of making a so-called shelter magazine, I always felt
clear-eyed about how things stood. To give you a glimpse of the
sorts of things designers put up with: Its perfect madness came
home to me on September 12, 2001, when a decorator called me
in tears because one of his clients on Manhattan's Upper East
Side had berated him for an hour as he tried to explain why her
new sofa cushions could not be delivered that day. I spent more
than a decade in the belly of the beast of muchness and more.

The folding of the magazine was ruthless. Without warning, our world collapsed. No one was expecting it. I came to
work on Monday, went to the corporate offices for a meeting, got

the news, and was told to have everything packed up by Friday. Within five minutes I was getting phone calls from media writers outside the company; they heard the news before I could get back to my office to tell my colleagues. Security guards were posted; I wondered if there was management concern about the fate of all those wildly expensive bolts of fabric in our prop closet.

"Fabric? Who cares about fabric?" said one guard in response to my question. "We don't want anyone kicking in the walls. Or taking computers."

I had to laugh.

In the four days we were given to pack up our belongings, I was overwhelmed with an urge to hoard, and began stuffing every *House & Garden* paper bag, pencil, and notepad I could get my hands on into a box, so that I would never run out of office supplies. I salvaged enough to run a small corporation from my kitchen. I didn't think of this as stealing. I thought of it as a twisted sort of recycling, for me, and for the stuff—part of the strange new economy of severance into which I had been thrown. Everything with our logo on it was destined for the shredder anyway.

Even so, a few weeks later I realized I had some gaping holes in my inventory: I had no ink for my printer. The pages of my résumé looked faded, ghostly. You would have thought I was fading too, but I wasn't. I was getting plump. All I could think about was food. This was the beginning of being hungry all the time. My addled brain was interpreting the white noise of unemployment to mean that I was going into hibernation, so I had

to fatten up to get through the long winter ahead. After the closing of the magazine was announced, my public line was: "I had a
great run; I took a magazine from zero to 950,000 readers in ten
years, won awards, published four books . . ." I was a zombie.
"Great run . . . 950,000 readers . . . four books . . ."

But privately, I was in a whiplashing tailspin. My nightmare
had finally come true. For years, I had had a profound dread of
unemployment that went way beyond worrying about how to
pay the bills. I would like to say that this was because of the inse-
cure nature of magazine publishing in general, and life at Condé
Nast specifically, where the backstabbing at the highest levels of
management was elevated to an art form, an elaborate corporate
kabuki. But actually my anxiety had more to do with my own
neuroses. Work had become the scaffolding of my life. It was
what I counted on. It supported the structure. Work held up the
floor of my moods, kept the façade intact. I always worried that
if I didn't have a job, I would sink into abject torpor. I couldn't
imagine life without work—or, if I did, I went cold with fear. Not
for me, those fantasies of sunny days at the beach.

I have always had a job. I have always supported myself.
Everything I own—my house, my piano, my kayak, my trees—I
purchased with money that I earned. For the thirty years I've
been an adult, I have had an office to go to and a time to show up
there. I've always had a place to *be*, and you can read as much existential gravitas into that as you want; there's plenty there. I had
never even changed jobs without having another job lined up.
It was probably compulsive not to spend a few days in between

jobs quietly thinking about what I would like to do, rather than just leaping into what others offered me next—but this problem afflicts many of us, sort of like not leaving a bad boyfriend until you have a new boyfriend lined up. It feels safer. Without work, who was I? I do not mean that my title defined me. Whatever status came with being an editor at Condé Nast didn't mean much to me; it seemed silly, overblown, something that other people projected. What did define me was the plain old simple act of working. The loss of my job triggered a cascade of self-doubt and depression. I felt like a failure. Not that the magazine had failed, but that I had.

I needed a job to do. I thrived on deadlines. I wanted my attendance to be required. I wanted reasons to stay in touch with people, good reasons like monthly corporate meetings and budget meetings and circulation meetings, weekly meetings with product designers and decorators and architects, daily meetings with editors and writers and photographers to generate story ideas, sales calls with publishers to generate ads, speeches and television appearances to generate publicity. Work even dictated my social life. Every night, if I chose to attend—and often enough, attendance was mandatory—there were openings and parties and lectures and dinners. I am not a very social person. If anything, my natural state is solitary, so this was the hardest part of my job, but at least it kept me out and about. I hired people who reveled in high society, with its patronage of design, to compensate for my shyness. They would bring photos back to the office, and with me safely behind the scenes, we would choose what to feature.

SLOW LOVE   13

The thing about running a magazine is that there is always so much to do. One deadline is met, and another rolls in right behind it. But editing the magazine was only the beginning of the job. The days of walling off editorial from the business side are long gone, if they ever existed at Condé Nast; editors are expected to sell ads, and to participate wholeheartedly in marketing events. Publishers seem to claim the right—and indeed, are expected to deliver—editorial coverage of their important clients. Editors who don't respond put their jobs at risk. When Giorgio Armani demands coverage for his collection or he'll pull his lucrative pages, guess what's going to happen? Editors are also expected to generate publicity for themselves as much as for their magazines. It doesn't matter if the gossip is negative, so long as it is boldfaced.

There is no such thing as corporate camaraderie. It is every publisher for himself, all pitching the same advertisers, and asking them to pay premium prices for our pages. The pressure is unrelenting; we went through five publishers in ten years; the turmoil was unimaginable. And every editor is on her own, too. No such thing as calling someone who knew the ropes to get advice; no such thing as a colleague to bounce ideas off of. For that matter, for thirteen years I could count on my colleagues to start rumors about me—that I was about to lose my job—every six months. And that elevator full of fashion snobs! It is legendary: how you're looked over, head to toe, by flocks of beautiful, mean girls, their needle-stung lips puckering in disdain. I felt as if I were surrounded by flights of gazelles on a savannah, strange, exotic creatures. One punishing winter, it was mysteriously decreed that legs had to be bare, and I watched as haughty women, bowing to the pressure of the herd, stalked in to work on stilettos, shivering with cold, their flesh attractively mottled and goose-bumped.

Over the years, many of our advertising clients remarked that they were stunned by the competitiveness of the company, and while they were drawn to the glamour of the parties we would throw for them, they were offended by the gossipmongering. While the company lifestyle is lavish, the company culture is fearful. The day I started, the editor of *Architectural Digest* announced to the press, "I killed that magazine once, and I'll kill it again." I felt as if I had walked into *Grimm's Fairy Tales*. She wasn't the only one gunning for us, but she was the only one vulgar enough to dance publicly on our grave, when she announced at a design industry dinner her pleasure that we were gone and her decision to blacklist from her pages anyone who had supported us. It seems petty, but it was punitive for designers, who run small businesses and cannot afford to advertise their skills; magazine features are the only way to demonstrate what they can do to a wide audience of potential clients.

All of it was perversely fascinating, so long as I could maintain a skeptical distance. I tried to keep my colleagues away from the culture of gossip and backbiting, partly by hiring from outside the company, and partly by not tolerating it within our offices. It certainly took a toll on me; I couldn't begin to count the number of evenings I went home and collapsed in exhaustion over yet another round of political savagery. The only way

I could survive was to toughen up, just ignore it all, and do my best work.

We walled ourselves off as best we could, and within *House & Garden*, we enjoyed years of stability. Some of us were together for more than a decade. We formed a sort of office family; we spent more time with one another than we did with our own families, and we were united in our simple ambition to make a beautiful, informative, well-written magazine that would teach readers about the design world. The flip side of being part of the high-strung stable of thoroughbreds owned by a mercurial boss was that editors in chief were given freedom to be inventive about their subjects. We had generous budgets for writing and photography. The corporate zaniness seemed a small price to pay for the opportunity to create my own magazine; that doesn't come along too often in an editor's life. Besides, I liked *not* being in control of my time, no matter how much I might have whined about it—that meant I was always busy.

I thrived. I couldn't even do one thing at a time; I had to multitask in order to focus on anything at all. In some ways, I was extraordinarily productive. Because *House & Garden* was a monthly magazine, our deadlines for getting pages to the printer were months ahead of the date on the cover of the issue. So, for example, we would be working on the September issue in May. That meant we were never operating in real time—it might have been late spring in the world, but in our everyday working lives, it was fall. I always felt out of step with the seasons. Eventually, I wasn't even living in real time. One Saturday in June, after a grueling deadline for the September issue, I asked my younger son how he had enjoyed summer camp. "I haven't gone yet, Mom." Of course. I knew that.

With the closing of the magazine, my beloved family of colleagues was obliterated. And so was the structure of my life.

Within hours of leaving my office for the last time, I can hardly bring myself to care about my résumé, or my reputation. I just want to eat. I begin calling every employed person I know with a job to take me to lunch. I want to fill my calendar with the promise of meals, days and days of them, even if they are only penciled-in promises—this, after all, being Manhattan. Only food can ward off the rage, fury, despair, and raw fear that have overcome me.

During my first post-employment lunch, my panic about not having a job is full-blown. When the waiter comes bearing bread, it is all I can do to keep myself from wrapping a dozen breadsticks in a heavy linen napkin and tucking them into my bag. I float the idea, actually, and my companion laughs slightly, nervously, gauging the level of my seriousness. I manage to control myself. He is an enormously appealing, calm, funny, brilliant person who knows a lot about business and politics, so nothing in the world surprises him, and he sees a way to market oneself right out of every disaster. He is a good friend, and gives me loads of advice, which I hear through my frantic chewing. I do feel better. I eat a huge amount of food. I end the meal extracting a promise of several more meals in the future; I want meals with friends bearing menus.

Panic hangs heavily about my shoulders for the next few weeks. How had I managed to get this far in my life completely unprepared for the unknown—which I had always known was out there? The unknown: what is going to happen today? What am I going to do? My friends begin to worry, and to make koan-ish statements like "No one gives a crippled crab a crutch." I take riddles like that as distractions, turning them over, the way a child takes a rattle in its fist.

I begin keeping notes about how I am feeling, what I am doing. Writing has always been my way to absorb things; I often write out my troubles. It even crosses my mind that maybe this will be the time in my life when I finally have a chance to write for a living. I know that it doesn't pay well, but I figure if I combine it with some consulting work, I could support myself. Luckily, or wisely, I had not changed my lifestyle while I was working at Condé Nast, so I had saved money. This was just before the stock market and the publishing business fell through the floor. Little did I know how frightening things would become.

But I quickly develop a strange problem with my typing— and I am a world-class typist. I notice that I keep mssng the *i* key—thngs kept comng out without t. Strange. I know there is no neurological pathology in the middle finger of my right hand. I just can't strike the *i*. Mssng the *i* means retyping words over and over again. This goes on for weeks. It is a pain. I stop wrtng.

After a few weeks of being unemployed, I begin to settle into a routine—of getting up.

"Today is Saturday," I say to myself one morning. I repeat this several times, like a mantra, trying to convince myself to get out of bed. Saturday is what I have come to think of as one of the nice days, like Sunday—when I consider days at all. "Today is Saturday. No one is working today, so you are no different from anyone else," I say out loud.

In fact, I have found it hardly necessary to be aware of what day it is. One of the pleasures of a workday morning was to rise early, have a cup of tea, walk through the garden, and get to the train on time, where I could read the paper front to back. Now that I do not have to get to work, I no longer have a structured time to read the daily paper, so I stack it into a pile, thinking I'll get to it later, until I realize I am creating a weekly daily.

I miss Fridays especially. They once meant relief, relaxation, an end to the busy week, time for rest and housekeeping. Now every day is Friday. Or Monday. Whatever.

Time hangs heavily on the unemployed soul. I eat an egg at 8:00 A.M., and by 9:30 I am starving. I become obsessed with eggs, gazing on their refined shape in wonder. Perfect packets of nutrients. I eat eggs all day long. When I had a job, I never had to think about eggs. I become broody, producing nothing. And the more I eat, the hungrier I get. It is easy enough to understand the concept of comforting oneself with food, but the comfort part goes right by me.

I might be busy all day, and then, when I'm in bed again, realize I have done nothing. The last time I felt this way was when I had a newborn and was so exhausted from nursing through the night and keeping an eye on the sleeping infant all morning that I couldn't get into grown-up clothing until late in the afternoon.

For heaven's sake, I hadn't even thought of it as grown-up clothing since I was a five-year-old dressing for kindergarten. Unemployed, I can't think straight enough to figure out what to do, until I realize that the day has gone by and I have done nothing.

"How are you today?" my sister Nicole asks. She is worried, and she calls several times a day. "How was your morning?" my sister wants to know.

"Incredibly busy. Unbelievable."

"What were you doing?"

"Sleeping."

In this way, being unemployed is a lot like being depressed. I wish I could be expansive about the mental physics of it all; I simply know enough to tell you about time, energy, and motion. Time drags, when it isn't speeding past. This is relative to everyone else. Energy is unreliable and has a distinct bearing on motion. Ah, yes, something else hovers at the edge of my consciousness. Mass. That would be me.

Why is it that for the last ten years, when I most needed its healing balm, I was unable to sleep? And why now, when I have no reason to be rested, can I not wake up? For years I had tossed and turned, and been awake at 4:00 A.M., a miserable hour if ever there was one. Yet I could be bright and happy all day at the office. Now, I am sleeping for ten or twelve hours at a stretch, and still, when I wake, I am tired and cranky.

This undoubtedly has to do with chaos theory.

You know how there are millions (okay, a handful) of things you swear you would do if you only had the time? Now that I have all the time in the world—except for the hours during which I'm looking for work—to read, write, travel, take walks, play minor-key nocturnes, have lunch with friends, train a dog, *get* a dog, learn to cook, knit a sweater, iron the napkins, and even the sheets, I have absolutely no energy for any of it. Just thinking about it exhausts me. I am no longer a body in motion.

Entropy. There's a concept I can tell you something about. "A closed system," my dictionary says, "evolves toward a state of maximum entropy." I feel like a closed system, because I have lost my part in a living, breathing entity that was a function of all the quirks and passions and personalities of everyone I had worked with, gathered together. That brilliant organism, sparkling with imagination and effort and love, dissolved around us. We were left scattered, little unbonded atoms. I have absolutely zero experience in filling my days with activity of my own choosing. Being unemployed means being unoccupied, literally. I feel hollow. "Entropy is a doctrine of inevitable social decline and degeneration."

To which I can only add: me, too.

"Today is Saturday. Get out of bed."

It being Saturday means that I can feel a little bit normal. Saturday is not a workday. I rise early. I open the curtains to let in some light. The clouds have lifted; the sun is sparkling through the rich, late fall colors of the sassafras trees that fill the front yard. I remember how I had once loved Saturdays, how weekends had given me a heady sense of freedom. When my calendar had been crammed full of meetings, simply to have had a blank day was elating. Now, all that mattered was that everyone else's Saturdays were different from Mondays.

I make a breakfast of the leftovers from a post-employment lunch, and then I put on a hat and mittens. Did I mention that we were all fired just as the holiday season was upon us? So much for Thanksgiving. I head into the streets. The early sunlight is slanting across the shop windows. Everyone is hurrying past me. Suddenly I notice that the men on the sidewalk look strange; they are in overcoats and polished leather shoes, and carrying briefcases. The women are dressed up. They have introspective, determined, grim faces. Strange for a Saturday.

That's when it hits me.

Today is not Saturday. It's Friday.

2. FORAGING

AFTER A MONTH of unemployment, it has come to this: I am foraging for my dinner, at four in the afternoon. In my own kitchen. I have developed a habit of eating leftovers from meals enjoyed days earlier, and my breakfast of spaghetti and meatballs at dawn sickened me by noon. Before too long, I'm feeling hungry again, but balky, wary of my own housekeeping, which lets me down from time to time. Better to have a drink. Safer.

Normally I like a bottle of Guinness stout when I need a nutritional hit, but I've gone through my supply. I spot a nearly empty bottle of Lillet that has been moldering at the back of the refrigerator for a while. Sugar and liquor only improve with age, right? I empty it into an oversized breakfast cup and read the recipe on the bottle. A twist of lime? Who keeps limes? I throw in a slice of lemon. Then a few more. Half a lemon. Vitamin C. I like to rehearse the nutritional content of my food, and there are times when a drink qualifies as a meal. I take a sip, and it isn't half bad, or, I suppose, it's only half good. Note to self: next time, make an effort. Have a whiskey sour. More vitamin C.

I start to lift my glass in a toast, another habit.

"To nothing."

I think better of it.

"To life," I say out loud.

Then I give myself another one of my daily lectures: Buck up. Just because something has failed doesn't mean I am a failure. Just because something has ended doesn't mean it was all a mistake. Just because I have been rejected doesn't mean I am worthless and unlovable. Sound familiar? It would if you or anyone you know has gone through a divorce. I had hauled myself through that many years earlier. This feels like the same thing.

Worse. A divorce you choose. Unemployment chooses you.

Did I mention that on top of it all, I had spent the last decade getting in and out of a difficult relationship—over and over again? In the miasma of job loss, I am realizing that lost love is weighing me down. That affair once seemed equal parts delightful and complicated, but as we drew closer, it tilted ominously toward painful. We broke up two years ago, though we stayed in touch, and I never let go of the hope that things would change. That failure of love hangs heavily on my heart. I am nurturing a budding rescue fantasy: maybe this time; because I really need him to, my charming prince will come through for me.

My thoughts are morphing into those computer clouds of aggregated words. Two big bubbles pop up: Work. Love. The two most important things in life, Freud had said. So, I was down two for two.

Then a third blob pops into view, nudging everything else out: Food.

Drink in hand, I decide it is time to wash the windows on the second floor. I could use a little exercise. Funny how sugar works: suddenly a surge of energy. Cleaning is an activity I have thrown myself into these days. I may be a mess, but at least I can control the mess in my house.

"How are you today?" my sister asks. She is down to calling twice a day. Cleaning has also enhanced my conversational repertoire; my sister seems enthralled by all the activity.

"How was your morning?" she wants to know.

"Incredibly busy. Unbelievable."

"What were you doing?"

"Vacuuming."

I get a big sponge out from under the sink, fill a bucket, and climb the stairs to my bedroom. A few more sips of the Lillet to fortify me for the job, and my mind is racing. I have always been a cheap date. This time it only takes one drink, and I hit bottom. As I reach for the corner with my sopping sponge, sucking on the lemons at the bottom of my cup at the same time, I imagine that the casement has snapped under my weight.

I watch myself fall out the window. I watch my cup shatter on the flagstone.

Or do we land at the same time? What was that about the feather and the cannonball being dropped from the tower? Where was that? Pisa? Didn't I go there? Was that on my honeymoon?

I look down from the window and see myself splayed on the stone terrace, my back cracked and spine twisted—like the lime that's supposed to be in my drink?—my head resting at a birdlike angle. This is where they (who?) will find me four days later, when it occurs to them (who, though?) that I haven't been seen for a while, haven't kept an appointment (do I have any?), and haven't called the children.

The children? I can't help it. I think of Alex and Theo as children still, though they are grown and out of the house. My thoughts suddenly flash on my older son, and I wonder what his life will be like. He met his first crush when they were toddlers, one mother pushing a stroller toward the other mother pushing her stroller. Even I—who as a rule didn't notice other people's babies, being freaked out enough by mine—paid attention to this one: tight marmalade curls poking out of a pink knit cap trimmed with pale pink feathers surrounding her bright, white, smiling face, a wisp of a ponytail hanging from a hole cut into the back of the bonnet. My usually reserved two-year-old son took one look at this rare bird and, standing straight up on the foot bar of his stroller, chortled, crowed, and clapped his hands so hard that he lost his balance, toppled over the restraining bar, and fell on his face at Sophie's feet—or rather, at her wheels.

That was Alex. He has always known what he is about, in the most straightforward fashion. When he was four or five, he marched up to his father and me one evening.

"When I grow up, I am going to marry to Mom."

"But Alex," his father said, "I'm already married to Mom."

"Don't worry, Dad. You'll be dead by then."

My theory is that Alex learned early that he was capable of falling hard, and thus learned almost as early how to protect himself. This trait, I am constantly reminding myself, was revealed long before his parents got divorced, so it isn't our fault. I suppose it isn't even a problem. It is just alien to my way of going through life, but I'm trying to learn from him. He is one of the most well-defended people I know. When he was four, he came to the hospital to meet his new baby brother dressed in full, red-coated Nutcracker soldier regalia, leaving his toy rifle at the door only at the request of a startled nurse. He attended his first day of kindergarten wearing a Ghostbusters uniform, complete with goggles, vacuum hose, and tank for storing phantoms strapped to his back. Ten years later, preparing for his first trip abroad, he memorized the Paris Metro map and knew how to navigate the city before he got on a plane. He studied a book of the architectural history of his school before he left for college. Now he is in law school, where there are infinite rules to learn and to create.

Alex calls every Sunday, charmingly, sweetly punctual. My younger son, in college, barely acknowledges a message. Theo does not believe in making a call unless he has a specific and necessary reason to do so. It has not yet occurred to him, still in that way a child, that his mother's need for him might be its own best, most specific and necessary reason to call.

So, I reason, the children are not going to be the ones to find me broken-necked on the terrace. Frankly, no one will. I'll rot.

I decide I am in no condition for housekeeping this evening, and drop my sopping sponge into the bathtub. I've watched myself hit bottom. That's what you have to do to get better, right? Anyway, I'm hungry. For a change.

There are three jars of peanut butter—protein!—on the

shelf. I don't even bother to find my reading glasses so that I can choose the freshest jar, but I take down a dessert plate, just to maintain standards. I fish around in the utensil drawer and find a spoon, unscrew the lid, and dredge deep into the jar. I dollop the stuff generously onto the plate—an extra helping so I don't have to come back downstairs for seconds. I put the plate of peanut butter, a half bottle of wine, a glass, and a linen napkin on a tray, and climb back up to my bedroom.

A few years ago a friend who is a chef told me that her guru said one should never do anything else while eating. Be present with the food. Pay attention to it. Honor it. Be thankful for it. Taste it. Savor it. Sit at a table. Light candles. No book, newspaper, or magazine propped up near the plate. No standing at the counter, or in front of the refrigerator, or, worst of all, over the sink, since that's where the plates are headed anyway.

But this evening I might have been better off reading a book while eating my peanut butter. Without the distraction, my thoughts circle around lost love. I am longing for safety, stability, security. Somewhere deep inside, under my tough feminist hide, I still believe in fairy tales. I *need* to believe in them. So I haul my charming prince out of the dungeon of my heart where I've been keeping him, brush him off, and give him a hopeful little nudge.

Never mind that I should have known better every time I returned to that troubled relationship—and I often returned over the course of many long years. Never mind that I ignored all the signs, or, worse, thought I could change things. Never mind my wise friends, who warned me that the relationship would never work. Never mind the psychic—I had come to believe in the predictions of psychics, clairvoyants, numerologists, astrologers—who had riffled through her brightly colored cards, pulling up the Tumble from the Tower of Death, the King of Swords, the Hangman, the Wheel of Fortune, turning, turning. . . . I recall the tarot reader sweetly, sternly abandoning her cards, lowering her glasses, and peering only into the future present, which lay shrouded somewhere in the vicinity of her kitchen table, asking me, "What is this big stone house he has in the country, that he goes to by himself? Who is this man who disappears constantly?"

How did she see this stuff? Was she talking to my sister?

She riffled through the cards, and more alarming figures fell to the table, characters bearing swords and hammers, tumbling from crumbled towers.

"He is incapable of change. Give him up. He will bring you sorrow. Give him up."

Who listens to the reasonableness of the irrational?

And so our affair unfolded, with all the frank recrimination and fugitive pleasure, all the joy and resurrecting power of love. How could that have been a mistake? And it unfolded as foreseen by the psychic, a Sicilian woman exactly my age, living downtown in her sixth-floor walk-up, with the tub in the kitchen and the cracked, stained teacups on hooks over the sink, cat snoring on the table in a milky pool of sunlight, the straggling plants smudged with ash on the fire escape, the refrigerator buzzing and humming. The cat always jumped on the table when a reading turned to love, the psychic said, stroking it. Or trouble, she added, arching her eyebrows at me.

I wasn't the first woman to have an affair with an ambivalent man. But even with the cards flashing like neon signs— DO NOT GO THERE—I was uncontrollably drawn into that relationship.

Through the clouds of grief I'm sitting in this evening, I spot another benefit of having had a job: it was always there, faithfully demanding my attention, regardless of my love life. Work more than filled up my time. It kept me distracted from painful questions, such as: Do I really want to spend the rest of my days tethered to ambivalence?

The peanut butter is sticking in my throat, and I am descending into that state of mind where even a bad relationship looks appealing. Better than nothing, nothing being how I feel. Tonight I am in the rapids of memory. I am desperately missing...well, I was going to call him Walker, as that's what he did best: walk away. But he didn't like that name when I told him that I was writing about him. He suggested "Stroller" instead.

"As you know," he said, liking nothing better than telling stories, even if he had to make them up, "the name came about a few generations ago when my family made a small fortune creating a special spring mechanism for baby strollers. Its novelty lay in providing two seemingly incompatible benefits: it allowed for greater stability when the carriage was being rolled along, and at the same time introduced a slight rocking sensation that relaxed the infant."

The operative term here is "infant," but in so describing himself, Stroller can lay claim to a breathtaking, even defiant, self-awareness. That doesn't mean he is going to do anything with his enlightenment, though. Come to think of it, strolling fits the pace of change in his life pretty well. Crawling would be more apt, but who names a lover Crawler? Stroller is the kind of fellow who takes his large, battered leather book bag to the beach, just to prove that he is not a baby, not afraid of the water—and not really there with you anyway. Plus, he would remind me, it contains his radio so he can listen to the ball game, when it isn't being interrupted by the noise of the waves.

Just thinking about Stroller I feel the anger rise in my throat. It's too early—and too late—for that. I once believed in the redeeming power of love. I once believed that it could heal all wounds, release the grip of childhood trauma. I'm no longer certain. Now I wonder if all we were doing was replaying old patterns, long ingrained in our characters, mirrored feelings of abandonment, rage, confusion, despair—and finally, clinging to fantasies of salvation, hope that there would be one person to take us to a happily-ever-after place.

What a glad heart I once had, whenever I returned to the pleasure of Stroller's company, after the coruscating anger of yet another fight had worn off. No matter how long it had been since our last encounter—six days or six months—Stroller and I always had a formal and lengthy dinner. We both needed a long passage from strangeness to intimacy. We needed time to unwind from the tension of separation and anticipation. I think back on dinners with Stroller, the playful, seductive conversation, the sprightly movement from one subject to another, the intense, passionate focus when we alighted on something that resonated for each of us. When you first meet someone, you can get an idea how lovemaking will be by how fluently your conversation moves.

Somewhere into a bottle of wine, Stroller would lift his glass to me, his face softened, the cares of the day drained away, his eyes tender.

"There is always a line," he said one evening, holding up his goblet so that the candlelight flickering behind it made the ruby tones glow. "There is always a line on the bottle. I cross that line, and I am overwhelmed by love for you."

"So the wine is talking?"

"It isn't the wine that makes me feel love. But the wine lets me be overcome by it. If I felt this way all the time, I could never get anything done. I can't be with you all the time. I would be weak with longing. I can contain my feelings for a while, when I see you, and then they spill over, and I must tell you how very much, how very deeply, I love you."

I began to notice that the line on the bottle was never in the same place from night to night. It was unpredictable. Sometimes he crossed it within a few sips; sometimes it took a few glasses. I began watching his face for telltale signs that he was near the line, studying the softening of his gaze, the pace of his breathing, searching for signs of release.

"I never know where it is," he told me when I questioned him. "It is elusive. I never even see it coming. But it does. There is always a line on the bottle."

How could I not fall in love with someone who said things like this? Unless, of course, it was with someone who didn't need a line—or, for that matter, a bottle—to overcome his resistance to love. But that never occurred to me.

This evening's glass of wine tastes horrible with the peanut butter, but I drink it anyway. Even my child had seen the pattern of my life better than I had. I remember a day Alex was home from college, making himself breakfast, while I was sitting on the floor organizing old pictures and letters from a large trunk.

"Look at these letters," I said, pulling out some old typewritten, onionskin pages from a long-ago love who was still a good friend. "Isn't it wonderful how he expresses himself? What a sweetheart." Don't ask me what I was thinking—using love letters to give my son a lesson in creative writing? Teaching him how to treat women? I fished out a few more.

While Alex read the letters, I drifted into a reverie about my first boyfriend in New York—my first serious love, my first steps into my grown-up life, my own apartment, my first job. He had refused to own a telephone, which meant that if I wanted to see him I had to take a subway downtown. His apartment was about as far from mine as was possible without being on a houseboat, and his neighborhood was rough. People forget, or don't realize, how insane Manhattan was in the '70s. Often, I would ring the buzzer for a while until I realized he wasn't home, and then I would have to find him and his friends in the smoky din of CBGB. One night, when I hadn't been able to track him down in any clubs, I went back to his apartment and rang again. Still no answer, but I roused his next-door neighbor, a friend of ours. I begged him to let me come up and wait. After half an hour or so at Tom's place, I was getting impatient.

"Why don't I just let myself into his apartment?"

"Are you sure that's a good idea?" Tom said, raising an eyebrow in alarm.

"Sure. It'll be a nice surprise."

The problem was that Tom didn't have a key, so the only way for me to get into my boyfriend's apartment was to climb out Tom's back window to the end of the fire escape and creep along a ledge (five stories up), then pry open his window to climb in. Only passion makes us so stupid. The brick was rough against my face. Tom was hanging out his window, guiding me along—"Just a few more steps! You're almost there!"—wild with worry that I would lose my footing.

When I got inside, I washed some dishes and tidied up, nice girl that I was, then lay down in the bedroom to wait, and fell asleep. An hour or two later, I heard the key turn in the lock and heard his voice. He was talking to someone. And she was laughing. I was trapped. I considered hiding in the closet, but I had no time. I greeted them. The woman was some sort of Norse goddess, tall and blonde. Few would describe me that way. Under the circumstances, my boyfriend was a real gentleman. He kindly walked me down five flights of stairs and put me into a taxi. Hence the next day's letter.

Was it possible that my pattern of dating unavailable men had begun that long ago?

Alex put the letters down, scowling.

"Yeah, Mom, really good. These are really well-written letters. You fall in love with guys who write you great letters, but they're always about how sorry they are for the way they treated you the night before. How about a guy who doesn't have to write you beautiful letters apologizing for his behavior?"

Ahem.

So much for memories.

I'm done with my meal; there's a limit to how much peanut butter even I can eat in one night. All that's left of the wine is the dregs. The problem with dinners like these: no nutritional value. I'm depleting myself. I really must get a hold of things. Tomorrow I'll drive to the grocery store. I'll grill a steak. I'll toss a salad. I'll set the table. I'll stick to one glass of red wine.

But first I'll prop Tolstoy up at the table—so I can read about Anna Karenina throwing herself under a train.

3. FARMERS' MARKET

WITHIN THE FIRST month of unemployment I manage to establish a rhythm of reasons to get out of bed, and a way to keep track of time. I have one errand for each day: Monday, milk. Tuesday, walk. Wednesday, books. Thursday, walk. Friday, chicken. Saturday, walk. Sunday, cookies. The trick to this is that it doesn't really matter what day it is. The important thing is to vary the activity. Book day is especially good, because when I get to Barnes & Noble I can just join everyone else, wrapped in coats, lying around on the floor or propped up against the wall, reading. It is as quiet, busy, and comforting as a library.

An errand always gets me going, no matter what my mood. And getting out of the house is becoming a priority. I have become latched to my computer. I cannot log off. Only the heartsick and the unemployed are online all day long, staring at the screen even when nothing is coming into the mailbox. I couldn't keep up with my e-mail when I had a job, there was so much of it, thousands of messages a day, much of it spam; I had so little time for it. Now that I have plenty of time to maintain a hearty correspondence with anyone, few people seem to need to talk. Where did everyone go?

I can see the appeal of starting a blog, just to hear the sound of my own voice, but I'm afraid, as depressed as I am, that it would be the sound of one hand clapping. Terrified of losing contact with the world, I start spending hours on the Internet. I follow a group of bloggers whom I have begun to think of as my new colleagues. Reading their posts is almost like being in a conference room before a meeting: everyone has an opinion about what's going on; personalities and egos sparkle and clash in a free-for-all across my screen. And the best part? No meeting! You can delete, move on, ignore, scream, throw things, and no one can see you. The problem with my new community of bloggers is that there is no focus, no agenda, no narrative, no point. No place to stop. Everything is a digression from everything else. My mind begins to move in this fractured way, lighting on whatever catches my interest, leaving quickly before I have to concentrate. I am no longer thinking straight. I become blog-brained.

I cannot stop trolling the Internet. I tell myself I'm looking for jobs, and I am indeed trying to get into reset mode, deciding my life in magazines is all over, scrolling through foundation job postings. But I'm also diving for sheer dreck. Hours go by. I couldn't care less about movie star gossip, but suddenly I'm mesmerized by their diets, their drugs, their babies, their karma. Then I become obsessed with what is going wrong in the world. Basically, everything. I am becoming massively informed about climate change, which has long been my number one, trumps-all candidate for The Biggest Problem Humankind Faces, but the more I know, the more clearly hopeless the problems seem. This is not helping my state of mind, which is getting darker and more anxious. I begin to understand why adolescents tend not to follow the news. Life is hard enough, and it takes a mature strength of mind and character, both of which I am decidedly lacking, to handle what's going on without the filters of self-esteem.

One Saturday morning (at least this time I am pretty sure it is Saturday), a ray of sunshine penetrates the gloom and I wake contemplating a variation in my outings: a trip to Brooks Brothers, my favorite shop for nightwear. This is a manageable task. I couldn't bear the thought of going to midtown Manhattan on a workday, for obvious reasons, so Saturday is a good day for pajama shopping. This is an inspired errand, a nifty combination of getting me out of bed and prolonging my relationship with bed.

One of the most difficult tasks I have been facing every morning, once I am up, is actually getting out of my pajamas. I slip into them with the greatest ease. A few days ago, I was coming in the door at 2:00 P.M., having run the cookie errand, when my phone rang; a friend of a friend was calling to schedule a blind date (just what I needed, in my condition, but I had determined to mimic a healthy, outreaching attitude). I put the caller on speaker, and as the Speaker spoke, I stripped off my hot clothes, damp from a panic attack or too much sugar. As I was doing this, I was struck by the oddity of being naked before a Speaker I had not yet met. Never mind: he was living in Palm Beach. Even as one hand was peeling off tights, the other was reaching for the crumpled pajama bottoms I had thrown over the edge of the tub an hour earlier. The Speaker droned on. I was fully back in my pajamas by the time the Speaker paused; I was dimly aware that I had been asked a question, but had no idea what it was, so I commented on the unseasonably warm weather, always a safe bet in New York these days. I hung up with the mild discomfort of having not prepared properly for a test.

But how could I focus on a caller when all I could think about was getting into my pajamas? In my closet, the costumes of Condé Nast, the tweeds and silks and cashmeres, hung idly. I was glad to turn my back on them. I would be willing to place a large bet that I am the only editor who has ever been called into the CEO's office to be reprimanded because my publishers complained that I was not wearing enough designer clothing.

Well, most of that stuff was too tight now.

I have always had a thing about nightwear. I love it. I am attached to it. I hang on to it for a long time, moving the old stuff from drawer to drawer. Even when it is tattered, beyond all repair, I cannot bear to throw it away. From time to time I visit these drawers, and I bunch up the soft, thin fabric and bury my nose in it, letting memories come flooding back.

My nightwear, if it could talk, would tell you the story of my life. There, at the bottom of a drawer, are the beloved, billowing cotton flannel nightgowns of my girlhood. Lanz of Salzburg. The tags have curled and faded to discreet, blank strips. These gowns always, dependably, had eyelet ruffles at the wrists and the yoke, and two white pearl buttons up the back. When I got to summer camp I learned that you were supposed to wear the gowns backwards, buttons up the front, and never, ever buttoned. I can trace to Lanz of Salzburg my tendency, once I find a piece of clothing I like, to buy the same thing in six colors.

Those flannel gowns are the ones you are never supposed to wear once you have a man in your life. I was in Vienna once with Stroller when we stumbled upon an entire Lanz of Salzburg store. The trip had been fun, but somewhat fraught; I suppose traveling has its own way of bringing up neuroses, which must be why people say that you can learn everything you need to know about someone by taking a trip together. I learned nothing. Stroller had asked me to organize our days, as he was no good at that sort of thing. As soon as I started plowing through guidebooks, I realized I was no good at it either. I had a secretary who prepared my agenda, dictated by sales calls and meetings. I took business trips. I had never actually taken a *vacation* trip.

But in anticipation of a few days abroad with Stroller, I persevered. I called my friend Alex, a pro at hitting the road, literally; off the top of her head she rattled off a dozen suggestions for where we should go, what we should see, where we should stay. I organized activities in various neighborhoods, so that we wouldn't miss anything famous or have to tromp all over town. By the time the plane took off, I felt smugly self-satisfied with my organizational skills.

Things moved along smoothly until the second afternoon. We were standing in the middle of some major Viennese *platz* when Stroller spotted a chocolate shop. He was a chocolate addict; knowing this, I had researched the very best chocolate shop to go to, and it was on our agenda. But it was not that one. The good one, the best one, was only a ten-minute walk from where we were standing. Stroller began to tug on my sleeve, making whimpering noises and pointing like a beagle at the shop.

"No, no," I said. "I know the perfect chocolate shop to visit—everyone says it is the best. It's only ten minutes away."

"But I'm hungry now."

"Just a few more minutes, please. It will be worth it." I heard an angry stomping of a foot and imagined (I hope) that I saw fists clenched in anger.

"You're such a Nazi."

That stopped me cold. I had become the German nanny of his childhood. And a Nazi. In Vienna, of all places, where such a thing is completely plausible. He crossed the *platz* to his chocolate shop alone, and I shuffled off, tears streaming, to mine. Did I think, what a jerk? Yes. But I also thought, What did I do wrong here? Am I too controlling? But he was the one who asked me to take control! Why did problems always have to be my fault? It is by such small degrees that we bury ourselves in self-doubt. Fortunately, I was not too upset to sample the goods at the proper chocolate shop, to which my feet had automatically led me. And which, by the way, is justifiably famous.

I traced this fight to our having stumbled on Lanz of Salzburg moments earlier. It perpetrated a breakdown of adulthood. We had to go in, of course. As soon as I got to the nightgown counter, I was in a swoon. All that flannel in its original birthplace. I think it unnerved him, bringing on mommy issues.

And so, back to pajamas. They are a balm for all life's woes—even better than nightgowns. I cannot recall when I first fell under their spell; it would be nice to be able to say a boyfriend lent me a pajama top one morning, like in a Ginger Rogers or Katharine Hepburn movie. At any rate, I have by now conducted years of research into pajama shopping, and the best pajamas for grown women come from the men's section of Brooks Brothers.

Here is why Brooks Brothers pajamas are the best, apart from the obvious stuff like cotton, lapels, pockets, and discreet patterns: drawstrings. There is nothing worse than pajamas that leave a funny pattern etched onto your body by the thick band of elastic at the waist—no, what's even worse is that the older you get, the longer your skin stays marked. Brooks introduces a new color, or a new variation on discreet stripes, every year or two, but they keep the style the same. Retailers respect a man's desire to buy the same thing over the years.

These days I am going through my pajamas at a fast clip. As the foundation of my unemployment wardrobe, they are getting too much wear and tear. And so it is that this Saturday morning I am contemplating a trip to Brooks for a fresh set of pajamas.

First, though, I have to do some food shopping, as even I have to admit there is nothing left to eat in the house. I am still hungry all the time, but I have not been able to rouse myself to do anything healthy about it. Cooking defeats me: the planning, the shopping, the chopping, the interminable layers of an artichoke, the knife edge against glistening muscle, the hours of waiting to eat. All I do is eat ingredients. I am not like my friend Sarah, who, when her husband is away, jumps on her bicycle and rides to the farm stand, returning home to make herself dinner, which she eats by candlelight. I believe the operative concept there is *husband*; she is in the habit of cooking for someone else, so it is easy for her to keep going. I regard her with the shock and awe one reserves for alien creatures in, say, the Galápagos Islands.

I awaken in time to catch the farmers' market in full swing. I don't see any point in putting on clothes, so I throw a jacket on over my pajamas and make sure not too much of the top is peeking out from under the hem. Naturally, I blend right in at the fruit stand, where everyone looks like they just got out of bed, and probably has. I decide to load up on apples, about the only thing available at this time of the year, unless you're the sort of person who knows what to do with a pumpkin—it is hard enough to get the stuff out of the cans—or worse yet, chard. I am feeling so aimless, so overwhelmed by the variety of stuff that I vow then and there to launch my mission to learn to enjoy cooking, and to be conscious of my food. The first thing I notice, in this new mind-set, is that nothing at the farmers' market actually seems to be organic. On the other hand, sitting as it is on tables right across the street, the produce does seem to be local. Is that good enough?

Suddenly I'm paralyzed in front of the apples. I begin to wonder if anyone in the locavore community has considered how difficult and boring it might be to eat only locally raised, organic produce *all the time*. I make a mental note to find a grumpy online discussion about this, and I start talking to myself in the blog voice that has been bannering my days. We're so dependent on the farmer's whims, to say nothing of the season. One moment we are liberating ourselves from the Costcos of the world, where we have to buy large boxes that we'll never see the bottom of, and the next moment we are committing six months in advance to buying from farms sides of beef and entire lambs and pigs—to say nothing of industrial-size freezers. I am as capable as the next foodie of swooning over the thimble-size blackberries at the local farm stand in August, but how am I supposed to deal with January, February, March, April, or May, when the stand is shuttered? Unless you live in Northern California, or Rome, you have to spend hours, every day, *sourcing* (a dangerous word) dinner.

I can see it coming: just as the wine cellar was the status symbol of the 1990s, the root cellar will be the status symbol of these times, and mommies across the land will spend August canning tomatoes and blueberries. Because let's face it, this is just like the 1970s. Remember baking your own bread? Throwing your own bowls? Yes, the complicated, labor-intensive life was worthier! It was even a feminist thing. I was right there, on the front lines, baking my own whole-wheat loaves and throwing my own teapots. If you think I exaggerate, you have perhaps not yet read the memo about hanging your wet laundry on the clothesline to dry—from the clothesline advocacy group Project Laundry List, now lobbying the government for a prominently positioned clothesline on the White House grounds. And who exactly is going to have to deal with this new, labor-intensive, food-sourcing chic? Women! Single or otherwise engaged.

At the farmers' market I root through the bins, looking for the apples that aren't wormy or brown—the ones that might have gotten the benefit of pesticide. I notice everyone else is doing the same thing, rejecting the natural-looking, pocked and pitted ones, even though the farmer holding an apple is patiently trying to explain that the black marks are damage from a hailstorm. No one seems to be buying it. But then I impulsively take a bite of one, and with the sharp snap of white flesh my crankiness about local food dissolves. Since when was I the kind of person who believes looks are everything? These are the apples of middle age: scarred, yes, but ripe and rich. I hold the apple in my mouth, and in a moment of bliss I have an epiphany: *This is worth the trouble*. So what if I have to eat apples for a month. I'm a creature of habit anyway. And then I think: *I have time for this*. The farmer smiles at the look on my face.

Things are going so well on the new food-consciousness front that I decide to venture further and stock up on items like milk and pasta. But within a couple of blocks, I develop drawstring problems. I should have tied a double knot. My pants are sliding down. Breathless, I pause in a doorway to address the dishevelment, and I realize that on top of it all I neglected to brush my hair. I worry for a moment that I might have gone too far with the pajamas thing. I glance around, furtively, like a trapped animal gauging her chances for escape.

In a flash, panting in that doorway, I see that I could never look out of place, no matter what I am wearing. In that moment I understand that I am no longer alone in the world. I have rejoined the living. All around me are people running their morning errands, loading up with groceries and newspapers and cleaning supplies, wearing yoga tights or baggy pants and long T-shirts. No one wants to change out of bedclothes.

All around me are people who didn't want to get out of their pajamas. They just aren't ready to admit it. Yet.

4. SUGAR HIGH

I AM BEGINNING TO feel like I am getting somewhere in the effort to take better care of myself. I am turning the corner—to the excellent bakery where I have become a fixture. Everyone knows that sugar is extremely useful for short-term bouts of happiness. Cookies are the most convenient little packages of pleasure ever invented. The only problem is how big this bakery's cookies are: the size of a small pizza. Such things add up. I have begun to skip dinner, or rather, to have a cookie for dinner, in order to justify the calories.

I am regressing to college days, when I invented the Crackpot Cookie Diet, the idea being that if you eat nothing but cookies for a few days, you could (a) be happy; (b) achieve nutritional balance by including oatmeal cookies in the menu; (c) cut down on the chocolate bars; (d) lose weight from the manic activity brought on by stoking a sugar binge; (e) cut down on the number of decisions you need to make in the course of a day; and (f) do better in class by staying awake all night to get your papers written. It always worked for me. But by this point in my life, I have forgotten that it was meant to help you lose weight, not alter your moods.

I always carry my cookie home sneakily, sticking my nose into the bag for a whiff of dark chocolate. Then I break the cookie in two, behaving in that fetishistic way of a junkie. Halfway into the chocolate chip, my heart begins to race. This is the time to get things done: the laundry, the vacuuming, the scrubbing of sinks and toilets, those housekeeping chores that keep me busy until bedtime, which is still a long way off.

I'm giving myself a jump start. I may as well connect myself to the bakery with cables. That window of frenetic opportunity begins to slide shut after about an hour, as my sugar high begins to lose momentum. This means it's time for me to eat the other half. At this point, I typically stop my chores to take my pulse.

I admit that I do this out of nostalgia as well. Stroller used to take his pulse all the time. He would stop in the middle of the sidewalk, pressing two fingers against his wrist.

"I'm losing beats," he would say, panic in his eyes. "Where are they going?"

"Stroller, Tolstoy writes about that spot on your wrist being where the glove ends. But he meant for a kiss to land there. Here, let me kiss it."

"I'm about to have heart failure. I know it. Let me lean against this building."

Of course nothing was ever wrong with him, nothing that a sniff of chocolate couldn't cure, so I began to carry some around in my pocket. As I crumbled little pieces off, Stroller would look at me fondly, his color and appetite returning.

"My heart will keep losing beats until it fully engages with yours," he would say sweetly, maddeningly.

This is what men do: worry about their hearts. Many people believe another organ concerns men more, but actually, up to a certain age, they don't tend to worry about that one. Their hearts are what they obsess about. Maybe for good reason, though men are more prone to give women heart attacks than the other way around. I learned a great deal about men from raising sons. As an eleven-year-old, my younger son, Theo, had the anxieties of an old man. He worried constantly about his weight, another thing all men do, though you wouldn't know it from the way they talk in public. Men are, basically, twenty times more sensitive, fragile, and vulnerable than women. Theo was always referring to his body as "the refrigerator" or "the bakery shop, full of rolls." I would try to reassure him that he wasn't fat, that he looked just fine. One day he suddenly lifted his shirt to show me. I couldn't help it. I gasped.

"See, Mom? See?" he began to howl. "You agree! You gasped! I heard you! You gasped!"

He had plumped up.

That night, after dinner, Theo took my hand as we walked to his bedroom.

"Feel my heart, Mom," he said. "It is racing. I am losing too many beats."

I put my hand on his little breastbone. I could not tell if his heart was racing. "Your heart seems okay to me, Theo. It seems strong, actually. You have a very strong heartbeat."

He went on to tell me that he was worried about how he would make enough money to retire. I told him not to worry, that I would support him for the rest of his life if he wanted. I know, I know, that isn't what a responsible parent is supposed to say, but how could I resist coming up with reasons to keep him home? But a guaranteed life salary was no reassurance to Theo, who snarled sarcastically.

"Right, Mom. And you'll pay my taxes when I'm sixty, too, I suppose."

Taxes? When had my worries become his?

I pointed out that there was something he could do about his weight if he wanted. He could stop eating French fries and bologna for lunch. He could stop eating rice and yams and bread and Vienna Fingers for dinner. But Theo's favorite foods were always sweet and white. It made no difference that we were trying to eat healthy family dinners. He just sat it out, in silent protest, until he could tear into plastic packaging.

In spite of myself, I became alarmed by Theo's anxiety. I put one hand on my heart, and the other on Theo's, and searched for the difference in the beats. I could hardly feel my own heartbeat, while his felt as fast as a bird's. But he was so much smaller than I was. How could I have known if his heart was really troubled?

He climbed into bed, pushing all his sheets off, complaining about the heat, his long hair getting in his eyes and sticking to his skin, his T-shirt too tight.

"Theo," I said, "it is time to get in shape. Time for a different diet. Time for exercise. If you feel unhealthy, you can do something about it."

Theo hated to hear that he could do anything about anything. That was not his mode of living in the world. He was actually very capable, but only after he geared himself up to a motivational pitch of anxiety.

"I am going to have a heart attack, Mom," he said. Theo was always rehearsing a litany of worries and complaints. The heart attack, I saw, was shaping up to be a new riff. "I know it, Mom. I can feel it. I have heartburn all the time."

At this news, I took him in my arms. "No, Theo, no. You cannot leave me when you are eleven. It's just like the runaway bunny. If you have a heart attack when you are eleven, I will become your soul and we will fly away together and find a healthy new heart to live in."

Theo looked up from his pillow, his eyes full of tears and love and childishness. He reached up for a hug. I brushed the tendrils off his forehead and raked his thick hair across his head. I rubbed his shoulders and pinched down the length of his fingers, pulling out the tension, and then I rotated his hands, bent from his wrists, first one way, then the other. He always found this routine to be soothing. He grew calmer, and announced that his heart had stopped racing.

"I think I'll have pancakes for breakfast," Theo said dreamily, and then drifted off to sleep.

How is it possible that that child now towers over me, a beanpole wearing skinny jeans, and has moved to California? He has girlfriends, and he breaks their hearts, or they break his—and it's all I can do to keep from calling their mothers to demand to know why their daughters are being so mean to my son.

And how is it that the child who never returned phone calls has suddenly become the person to check up on me, constantly? When I didn't have a new job within two months, it dawned on him that I was living out his childhood fears about houses and taxes, and he began to understand how lost I felt.

One day I told him about the Cookie Diet.

"Mom. That is not the way to be healthy. You have to let go of this. All desire leads to unhappiness. Nothing is real. It is all an illusion."

He had undertaken a new course of study in college, acquainting himself with Zen and the way of the Tao—

"Can I have your credit card number for a plane ticket home?"

The problem with the Cookie Diet is the Cookie Crash, a withdrawal that sends you right back to the bakery, to start all over again, trying to keep the bubble of energy aloft. What can I say? I approach food as I approach love, with reckless abandon. I get so hungry for sugar that I finally take my mixer out of the closet and start baking my own cookies. That way I can have something to nibble on in the middle of the night.

Not exactly the kind of cooking I had in mind when I vowed to take better care of myself, but a start. Dessert has always been my favorite course, anyway. It is an extremely rewarding pathway to kitchen mastery, and when things go wrong with cookies, they don't look or smell disgusting. I am feeling pretty good about my new endeavor. At least I am dusting off the old equipment. And, happily, the best outfit to bake in is an old pair of pajamas.

As soon as I put out the word that I am baking, my friends begin to send their favorite recipes. I start a professional-looking dessert file—what else could I do with all those office supplies? That file is getting fatter, too. I am becoming friends with a woman who is a potter and as passionate about dessert as I am. Frances called me after the magazine folded, and then—here's the difference—kept calling, to see how I was, to draw me out for a walk, or a talk. It was those second, third, and tenth calls that really moved me. She is kind and generous. She even baked a set of dessert plates and coffee cups in her kiln and sent them to me in celebration of my new cooking habit. The idea of filling my days with baking cookies, maybe even someday sitting at a potter's wheel, begins to seem incredibly appealing. So it took falling off the career track to find the time to make Guinness Stout Ginger Cake. How could I have ever wanted to live without that? Reading through the recipe, I understand what has been missing in my life. Balance. Time to get beyond ingredients.

It strikes me, as I read through another recipe from Frances—this one for Whiskey-Soaked Dark Chocolate Bundt Cake (note the soothing ingredient of alcohol)—that until now, I had not made a new friend in years. I don't know why, but I had gotten the idea that it is one of life's verities that one does not find new friends as one gets older. Now, I find that the opposite is happening. Some of my old friendships are deepening, though I have lost a couple of friends, too, due to the perverse pleasure some took in my pain. One actually shouted in glee: "You've lost your power! Now I can say anything I want to you!" I was dumbfounded. Had I really been so blind to her ambivalence? How had I missed her hostility toward me?

Now friends are reaching out their hands, and I am able to respond. And that, in turn, enables me to reach out to others when their worlds collapse, as is happening all around me. I rediscover a few key facts about friendships: They take time. They require attention. They need nurturing. Not the friends, necessarily, but the friendships. The quality and durability of any friendship reflects all that is put into it by both parties. Honest conversation. Availability. Sensitivity. Care. Compassion. Remember how our mothers used to talk about "having company over"? That usually meant a frantic round of vacuuming, and a competitive round in the kitchen. But now I like to think of the companionship in that phrase, and I like that I can have company over and actually feed them something, even if it's only cake or cookies and tea.

It is only a matter of time before Frances begins to push advanced recipes on me, things like Perfect Roast Chicken—way beyond my ken these days. But my house fills with the aroma of hot vanilla and sugar. I stumble on a recipe for spice cookies that looks appropriately festive for winter, a nice change from chocolate chips. Mine turn out looking exactly like the pictures in the cookbook, and this achievement gladdens my heart beyond all reason. It has never happened before. I clap out loud.

Somehow, with my mixer whirring in the warm, quiet kitchen, the windows dark and frosted with the cold night air, I am managing to comfort myself. I'm sure I have lost many beats during these crazy days of sugar highs, but I have never missed them.

Winter

*"It's more real to me here than if I went up," he suddenly
heard himself say; and the fear lest that last shadow
of reality should lose its edge kept him rooted to his
seat as the minutes succeeded each other.*
—EDITH WHARTON, *The Age of Innocence*

5. THE STROLLER FILES

THERE MUST BE a special floor in the lunatic asylum of life reserved for people who get into ambivalent relationships. Or, more specifically, for women who get involved with ambivalent men, as that is, to my knowledge, the more common dynamic. Most of us seem to have the skeletons of crazy relationships hanging in our closets.

What is an ambivalent man? I resort to *The American Heritage Dictionary*, as I do for answers to all of life's big questions: "ambivalence *n.* 1. the coexistence of opposing attitudes or feelings, such as love and hate, toward a person, an object, or an idea." If that isn't clear enough, try "2. uncertainty or indecisiveness as to which course to follow."

Reeling as I am from the loss of my job, I can't stop yearning for Stroller; I'm stoking that elaborate rescue fantasy. Stroller will finally come to his senses, realize how much he needs me in his arms, be grateful that I am no longer tied to a job that distracts me from him, vow to take care of me forever, and sweep me into his life.

What is wrong with me? Nothing, in a way. It seems natural to want the person you've loved for years to come through for you. And everything, in another, more realistic way. Stroller made it clear enough, through all those years, that his idea of commitment was dinner, theater, and a long weekend. Much more than that tended to unhinge him.

I feel compelled to review our history, mainly to remind myself of how crazy things were. I need a reality check. So I begin reading my old journals to retrace the course of our lives together and apart. What is wrong with him? As soon as I begin, a bigger question nags at me. What is wrong with me? Ambivalence is not a state of mind I find particularly comfortable. I think of myself as passionate and full of conviction. I want to figure out why I can't give him up. Perhaps I am tempted to fall back into the old heartache simply for the security of knowing I am loved, regardless of the consequences. I am attached to him. Or am I attached to the drama? It seems I cannot close the Stroller chapter of my life. I start buying books with titles like *How to Break Your Addiction to a Person*, though I have to sneak them out of the bookstore under copies of the more classic treatments of addictive relationships, like *Middlemarch* and *War and Peace*. Finally I decide that I am my own case history, and if I don't dig in to understand what I'm doing, I will be spending the years ahead in a vexing pattern of intimacy and abandonment.

Stroller and I kept breaking up and getting back together again for years. But even a separation that lasted for months didn't seem to make any difference in our ability to connect when we did find one another again. We could always get mileage out of the simplest things, such as talking about a movie or a story in the newspaper. In truth, the banal moments of the day are the most seductive to me. It is in the lighting of a fire on a cold morning, or in the pouring of wine and the pulling up of chairs to read together at the end of an afternoon of errands, that love really exerts its magic. The moments of easy domesticity are what I miss most about life with Stroller. The company: the pruning of lavender side by side in the garden, the gathering of roses, the fragrance of whiskey in his glass, the pile of books at his elbow, the cigar ash falling to the carpet—"My grandmother said it keeps away bugs," he would say, crushing the ash into the pile.

Stroller loved me. But he also hated me. He was sure that, if we got too attached to one another, I would destroy him, in some murky, existential way—not quite a *vagina dentata* thing, but close enough for discomfort.

Stroller's situation was so subtly strange that I didn't even know what was going on until it was too late, because I had fallen hopelessly in love. Let me recreate our particular Genesis; everything that followed turned out to be a variation of that story. Apart from the singularity of its detail, the saga will be familiar to many who have gotten into the same mess—and to the patient, exasperated friends who have had to help them out.

When I first met him—and yes, I'm afraid it was love at first sight, and across a crowded room, at that—he had been legally separated from his wife for a couple of years, with boxes of lawyers' files and judges' decrees to show for it. I'll say it again, for emphasis: legal separation. This was important to me because by then, years after my own divorce, I had grown wary of men who told me their marriages were on the rocks. Perhaps I had misunderstood, and they had been referring to their cocktails, as it frequently transpired that their own spouses had not yet gotten the news. Anyway, Stroller and I were at the glitzy opening for the new headquarters of an auction house, the kind of event I attended, reluctantly, as part of my job. We had both wandered over to a handsome, shiny vintage car in the middle of the room.

"Hop in," he said, as he opened a door for me. "Where shall we go?"

By the time the guide hurried over to shoo us away from the car, I was on my way to lost.

However, as I learned at the end of that fateful evening when I offered to give him a ride home in my own car on my way to the suburbs, Stroller was still sharing in an apartment with his wife. The highway of denial yawned open before me. I chalked up his unusual living arrangement to the typical Manhattan real estate squeeze. Isn't it awful how hard it is to find an apartment in New York, especially after you've broken up with your roommate?

After an exchange of letters (pen and paper, a charmingly old-fashioned way to communicate), I invited him to stop by and take a walk with me one weekend on the way to his house in the country. It was then that he wrote telling me that he was "only available on a contingent basis." The bulb flickered in my brain; as I recall, I wrote an angry poem called "The Contingent Heart" (I will spare you) and told him not to write back.

A year later, at dinner with friends, I saw Stroller in a booth on the other side of the restaurant. Once again, my heart lurched with attraction. On my way out I stopped to greet him; he was still as twinkly as ever. He had a knack for looking dapper and rumpled at the same time. He proposed we meet for lunch. We proceeded to meet for lunch every three weeks for the next year. These were jolly, rambling meals, a respite from the office for both of us, full of funny conversation fueled by terrific wine and delicious food. It was during these meals that I became fond of the elaborate rituals Stroller observed—removing his suspenders to sit down, tucking his napkin into his collar and spreading it over his tie and shirt, discussing the wine with the sommelier, and joking with the waiter about the issues of the day. It all seemed to be happening in the nineteenth century, my favorite time zone.

I would invariably stagger back to the office from lunch to find a phone message from my sister.

"How was lunch with the perfect man, *except he is married*?" she would always say. Emphasis hers.

"Perfect," I would reply. "And he is separated. *Legally*." Emphasis mine.

"Where is he living?"

"He is living with boxes and boxes of court documents. He pays child support. He pays alimony. He is legally separated."

My sister would remain unimpressed.

"There's no such thing as a free lunch."

Still, even after a year of lunches—and yes, in public; there was nothing to hide, that was part of legal separation—I kept my distance. Until one late summer day, it seemed not to matter that he was still living in the same apartment with his wife. For that matter, she no longer seemed to be home. We had dinner every evening for a week, and then we had long, winding midnight strolls through various strange and shadowy out-of-the-way bars downtown, and naturally one thing led to another. The perfect man seemed to be more committed to his legal separation.

We enjoyed a month of passionate weekends at his house in the country, which, he insisted, was not *their* house, just his. That, too, was part of legal separation.

He always returned to their apartment in the city. Somehow that had also become part of legal separation.

Then it was September 11, 2001.

I had never called him at home; I didn't even have his number. He never carried a cell phone. I had no idea where he was.

In retrospect, I realize I should have tracked him down and put an end to all the nonsense.

Several days later, we were having lunch again. Let me re-create the scene, as it tells of the banishment from Paradise, as well as the derangement of a howling Eve. Every event with Stroller over the course of the next few years was merely a re-play of this weirdly intoxicating potion of loving unavailability. Countless people have sampled it—some of us develop immunity; others, addiction.

"So, I'm thinking I should invite my wife to the country with me this weekend. Just to be safe. Something else might happen in Manhattan."

"So I'm *uninvited*? Why are you telling me this?"

"Full disclosure."

"Full disclosure? Full disclosure has nothing to do with us. Are you telling me this because you are warning me not to call you up there? Afraid I might cause you trouble? I don't want to know where your wife is, with you, not with you."

Stroller looked at me with such pity that I stopped.

"I'm sorry. This has upset me."

"I didn't mean that I wanted my wife with me in a conjugal sense. I meant it the way I would invite anyone who was staying with me, in my apartment in the city, under these circumstances. I would politely invite them to leave the city. What if something happens?"

"Why do you think something is going to happen this weekend, Stroller? Yom Kippur? Have you heard something? And what's going to happen uptown anyway? What an idea. That's the countryside, as far as terrorists are concerned."

"You're wrong. What about the theory that they'll blow up the Met? The country's cultural treasure chest? The heart of Western civilization?"

"The Metropolitan Museum of Art? Are you kidding me?"

Of course the whole city was on edge. No one had any idea what was going to happen next. No one knew if there were explosives hidden somewhere else, ready to detonate in the subways; there were rumors of suicide bombers and water supply contamination, and warnings to avoid crowds. And of course anyone would want to offer safe haven to his loved ones. The problem was that I had abandoned the rational world. And I had begun to consider myself one of his loved ones.

"Terrorists don't care about cultural institutions that are empty, Stroller. They care about Disney, and MTV, and Fox Studios. Do tourists walk around with pictures of the Met on their T-shirts? I don't think so. They walk around with the Empire State Building on their T-shirts. Times Square, Stroller. Where I work! Why don't you worry about *me* this weekend? Every day I take trains in and out of Grand Central Station. That's where trouble will happen, Stroller. That's where they're going to run a truck full of explosives into a building and blow everything up. Midtown. Not your goddamn uptown apartment building."

I took a deep breath. We were in a proper restaurant, doing our bit for the country by spending money, which, according to the president, was important. The place was nearly full. The wine had clearly loosened my grip on propriety; Stroller's feet were curled around my legs under the long white tablecloth.

I sat very still for a few moments, as if the storm might blow over.

Stroller was staring at me. He didn't say a word. That was a mistake. Nature abhors a vacuum, and so do I.

"I'm the one who will be blown to bits, Stroller. While you're holding your wife in bed in your room in the country, I'll be pulverized. And you won't even know it. You'll never see me again."

"Never mind. She's not coming. I'm not inviting her."

"Forget it, Stroller. Just forget it. I don't want to know whether she is coming or not. It is clearly none of my business.

A huge wave of jealousy has taken possession of me, that's all. You just have to see how this is from my point of view."

"I don't want to pursue this conversation any further just now, thank you."

"I agree. We were having a perfect lunch. Let's finish, and get back to our real lives, okay?"

"Okay, and she's not coming."

"I don't want to know, Stroller. Leave your options open. Wide open. That way you won't be lying to me if you wake up tomorrow morning afraid of terrorists and you have to leave town together."

Looking back over the beginning of our relationship, after enduring many cycles of breaking up and trying again, I'm somewhat horrified, and, yes, amused, to see that we kept repeating essentially the same conversation. I kept thinking things would change. I'm not the first woman to have been trapped in wishful thinking, and, sadly, I won't be the last.

We didn't drop the argument that long-ago afternoon. Over the next few days, Stroller vacillated between guilt over ending his marriage for good and his desire to be with me—and of course I had to hear all about it. At the same time, my sister, who had gotten wind of what was going on, had gone into full alert, code red.

"Do they still sleep together?" she wanted to know.

"I don't know. I don't know how big their apartment is, if they have separate rooms. I don't know anything."

"How big the apartment is? Who cares? I mean, *do they have sex*? Does he have sex with her?"

"How would I know?"

"You would ask him."

"No, I wouldn't."

"Why not?"

"I know enough about her already. Bad stuff."

"I would want to know all that stuff. "

"I don't want to know any of that stuff. I can't understand what is going on in that marriage. How is he so free? He leaves me and goes to sleep in someone else's arms, in another bed?"

"Maybe he doesn't. You could find out."

"Maybe he does. I would find out."

Everyone in my family was worrying about this mess, most of all me. As if our train had jumped tracks, in one short month Stroller and I were no longer having a relationship; we were in meta-relationship, arguing and elaborating and deconstructing. It was beginning to dawn on me that things were much more complicated in his household than he had let on. It was also beginning to dawn on me that I was kidding myself if I thought there was any happiness to be had in such a lopsided arrange- ment. After all, I was completely available. And besotted. "Legal separation" had turned out to be a term of marital martial arts. I was beginning to feel it would have been easier to have an old- fashioned, straightforward, sub-rosa extramarital affair. This situ- ation was murky and confusing—separation, independence, out in the open, legal papers, judges, custody, and alimony payments. But not divorced, not filing, not living alone, not budging.

"I'm giving myself a deadline," Stroller announced at din- ner the following week. "To decide what to do. It isn't good to drift. I have to decide. What kind of deadline should it be, do you think?"

I held up my wrist, and depressed the stopwatch function.

"Okay, Stroller. The second hand is sweeping around the dial. I am counting the seconds."

"Seconds?"

"You've had years to figure this out. What's a few more seconds?"

"I was thinking of something a little more ample. A lunar cycle, maybe."

"What's that? Where is the moon now? Are we going from half crescent to half?"

"How about Halloween?"

"That's more than a lunar cycle, Stroller, I'm sure of it. Half to full to half again."

"Halloween."

"Ghosts. Goblins. Witches. You want to do something important on Halloween?"

A vivid recollection of my ex-husband proposing marriage at a restaurant in Texas on Halloween flashed before me— as he announced that the time had come to make a decision, I glanced over his shoulder as a raucous parade of skeletons and freaks and monsters and goblins clutching beer cans and tequila bottles gyrated past the large plateglass window.

"Never mind, what difference does it make?" I said. "A lunar cycle and change. Fine. Halloween. And how exactly am I supposed to behave during this month, when I'm waiting for your deadline?"

"I don't know. I can't tell you that. You figure it out."

"Well, if I only have one more month with you, I'm going to enjoy it to the fullest. I'm going to get the most out of you. If you're going to break my heart in a lunar cycle, I might as well suffer then instead of right now."

"That's funny. I read an article recently—a scientist asked a bunch of men and women the same question: If you knew you were going to die, but you had the choice of dying immediately, or getting another five minutes to live and then dying, which would you take?"

I thought about this for a second. "I'd take the five minutes. What about you?"

"I would, too. But most men wanted to die immediately. Most women answered the way you did."

"You did, too."

"I'd want the five minutes so I could argue with the guy. The guy making the decision that I would die. I could change his mind. Maybe I wouldn't have to die."

"You're not allowed to argue, Stroller. That's the whole point. You're going to die. We're all going to die. You can't argue your way out of it. How do you use the time you have left? That's the point of the question."

Stroller had given me some blueberry-colored wool from the sheep that lived near his house, so during the lunar cycle, I began to knit him a scarf. Yes, I wanted to strangle him. We saw each other as much as we could. We cooked meals together; we danced to Cole Porter in the kitchen; we lit the first fire of the season one chilly night and watched from his bed as the embers glowed. The scarf was getting very long. We went to hear *La Bohème* at the Met. I began weeping as soon as the conductor picked up his baton. Stroller mopped my face with the large red rag of a bandanna he kept balled up in a pocket. At intermission we unwrapped the crinkly cellophane from a smoked salmon sandwich made with black bread and shared one of our favorite meals in New York City. You should only eat this sandwich at the opera. Stroller snuffled a stack of chocolate bars until he had inhaled enough to satisfy his sweet tooth. He was dieting.

The lunar cycle ended, and Stroller was still unsure about what to do.

We agreed to part.

A week later, my sister and I were at the opera again; this time it was *La Traviata*. Violetta would soon be dying, gasping for breath, for lost love, crushed under the weight of social opprobrium. She had lived her days alone, wasting away without the man she loved, and who had loved her but had given her up as an inappropriate liaison. Guess who was on my mind?

I glanced up from my program at the end of the second act, and there, as if I had magically conjured him up, was Stroller, threading his way quickly up the aisle. He always got out as fast as he could during intermission. He seemed to be alone—no, there was a gray-haired man walking next to him, a colleague? Stroller had probably gotten these tickets for us, I thought with tenderness, and then I had imposed the Lunar Cycle Decision. Shouting his name, in a most indecorous opera-house fashion, I clambered over the laps of the people sitting next to me, maneuvered past a hapless woman who was blocking the aisle while struggling awkwardly to get her arms into her coat, and raced up to Stroller, who had by then reached the exit. My heart was pounding with joy at the sight of him.

"Stroller! Wait! Stop! What a wonderful surprise to see you."

He looked dazed. He kept walking, and I matched his stride.

"Hello there," he said. His voice was dull. He suddenly stopped in his tracks, looked back, and froze. I turned to see the woman still struggling with her coat. She stopped in front of us.

"Meet my wife."

Thank goodness my mother had drummed etiquette into my heart. The habit of good manners kicked in; I shook hands politely and made small talk, ignoring the deranged screams of disbelief in my brain—let's just say I was not generous in my assessment. I left the opera and went straight to bed, trembling with chills, curled in a fetal position. I was sick all night.

Slowly, over the course of the next year or so, with heart-rending indecisiveness, Stroller eventually moved into his own apartment. I once would have said he moved at a glacial pace, but these days even glaciers moved faster than he did. In reality, Stroller had begun to straddle two lives. Still, there was progress, however deliberate and tiny the steps.

Was I sorry that I had gotten into such a mess?

Yes.

And no.

Ambivalence, you see, is contagious.

"Remember," my sister said repeatedly over the next few years, whenever I would go through another round of "do-si-do your partner" in my square dance with Stroller, "he still takes his wife to the opera."

6. SELLING THE HOUSE

I AM MAKING PROGRESS, moving from incapacitated to functioning, if barely. I am able to make calls, wrangle some freelance writing assignments, and get consulting work on a couple of long-term projects. For a few happy weeks, I even have a desk to go to, and a phone to answer, meetings to run. I am restored to busy health, until that job ends, too. Within months of *House & Garden* folding, the entire economy is in free fall. By 2008, advertising has begun to vanish from the pages of newspapers and magazines, layoffs and buyouts are announced, and there isn't much money to spend, at least on the likes of me. As winter settles in, with days so short and cold it hardly seems worth getting up at all, I am still without a full-time job. It isn't that I don't try. I meet with CEOs and editorial directors and headhunters at various companies. Nothing happens.

It is strange, and maddening, to be forcibly retired. Even the generational rhythms are out of whack. My father has retired! How could we have reached the same stage of life together? I am beginning to feel like an antique, an artisan whose skills are no longer even respected, much less needed. Writing? Editing? *How quaint*. Managing creative people? *We're only trying to manage to get rid of more of them.*

I decide it is finally time to sell my house in the suburbs of New York City. The stock market is sliding perilously, and I don't want to spend my life's savings on maintaining the mortgage and taxes. I want to be out of debt. I have been toying for years with the idea of moving out of that house, but as long as it hasn't been necessary to leave (and by now you may have picked up on the fact that some of us take a long, long time to make changes) I've been torn because the house belongs not only to me, but to the children, too. They refer to it as The Original House. It is a forthright, dark, wood-shingled, center-hall Colonial Revival, surrounded by gardens and nearly a hundred years old in a suburb that time has forgotten, though it is only eleven miles from midtown Manhattan.

I have been putting off the decision, but the time has come to say goodbye. A single woman—and exactly whose fault is it that I have gotten to this stage in life alone?—with grown children doesn't need a large house, even though every room is furnished and has clearly felt necessary.

It has taken me ages to create my home: twenty-two years, and all the years before that of daydreaming about how I wanted to live. This is the home I thought I would grow old in. It was supposed to be my Forever House—the house you think you will never leave, the house you love beyond all others, the place that is home, where you've recaptured only what made you feel safe and happy in your childhood home, and left the rest behind. (A variation of the vow we all made as girls: I will *never* grow up to be my mother. Never mind that these days I can't even begin to count all the ways in which I am like my mother, beginning with the vacuum cleaner clamped to my hand.) The Forever House is the place where you've passed along the values you admire to your own children, and in doing so, filled the rooms with laughter and tears.

I cannot step past the threshold of a son's room without becoming engulfed in memories, triggered by things as slight as the worn patch on the armchair where my arm rested while cradling a nursing child. This is the home I imagined my children would return to visit with their children, whose first steps would be taken in the garden, whose tiny fists would curl around the white azalea branches for support, just the way their fathers' had. I wish we still lived in a world in which houses were passed down through generations. But then again, I certainly wasn't about to move into my parents' house when I was ready to settle down. Why would I expect my children to do so? Our sense of home has become portable. That may be one reason we invest our possessions with so much more meaning—they, rather than rooms and gardens, have to carry the memories. What has taken a lifetime to create is about to be undone in a matter of minutes. Come to think of it, it's kind of like being blasted out of a career.

I call a realtor, an acquaintance in town who has always struck me as zippy and unflappable. She comes over immediately.

"I've *always* wanted to see this house," she says when I greet her at the door. I forget that because I edited a magazine about interior design, people assume I live in a decorator's palace. They are disabused of this notion as soon as they try to find the front door. The path has long ago been overgrown by thick, hundred-year-old azaleas. I like the romantic allure of the hidden, inaccessible entrance. I like the message too: Leave me alone.

"You'll have to cut those bushes back first thing," she says, waving at the front yard before she even enters the house. "People want a front door, you know. Most people."

So much for mystery. I never cared about what people wanted. Only what I wanted. This is, after all, my home. I have never been one of those people who run the resale equation before every change they make. I begin to see that this would have been a useful discipline. Instead I have spent years artfully, painstakingly pruning those very azaleas into their graceful shapes. I can tell that the realtor can tell that she has a character on her hands. And character doesn't sell.

We start in the kitchen because the realtor is able to find the kitchen door. Facing the stove is the oversized leather sofa on which Theo and Alex used to eat breakfast every morning, reclining in its enveloping depths. We called it The Boat. The sofa in the kitchen turned out to be one of my more masterful decorating coups; it inspired the upholstered armchair by the bathtub, and the bookshelves and ladder-back chair in the laundry room. Just looking at the sofa in the kitchen makes me tear up. I am fairly certain that it is not going to fit into my next house.

"Not to worry. It'll all work out. This is the hard part. Now, then, why don't you show me around?"

So we walk through the house, and I do my best to impersonate my concept of a real estate agent: "And over here is the laundry room, with bookcases built right in—"

"I've never seen so many bookcases!" the real real estate agent says. "You know, people don't want so many bookcases.

They don't even want libraries. They want media rooms. Where did you say the TV was? In the *dressing room*?"

I can almost see her mind whirring as she begins to figure out just what type of character she has on her hands. Hmmm . . . single, unemployed, not going out much, reading instead . . .

We walk through the kitchen. She eyes the walls warily.

"Interesting color. Very."

Isn't that what people say when they can't think of anything nicer to say?

"Oh, isn't that cabinet full of lovely things? My children made the same clay birds. You're going to have to put everything away. Everything. People don't like other children's art. You know, your kids are only cute to you. That's true about everyone's kids, by the way. Not just yours."

I show her the appliances, skipping the burner I meant to unclog a few years ago. When I open the cabinets, I notice, for the first time, how faded and stained the wood around the stove has become.

"This is terrific. What a gorgeous kitchen. You've decorated it so beautifully. Now you're going to have to clear all the counters. Vases. Books. Knickknacks. Get rid of all that stuff. I mean, it is just beautiful. Beautiful. I love what you've done with this house. Make sure you put it all away."

Did she just refer to my precious stuff as *knickknacks*? We walk through the living room, the dining room, the library.

"Have you actually *read* all these books? What an unusual color on the walls. What would you call that?"

I explain to her how I had been inspired by a bottle of old red wine, and how I'd taken a glass of it to the hardware store to get it copied. She raises an eyebrow. Funny, the guy at the hardware store had done the same thing. The character is coming into focus: single, unemployed, not going out much, reading instead . . . and drinking wine. Alone. At noon, no doubt.

"Gorgeous. All just gorgeous. Like I said, get rid of it all. You like photographs? I love your collection. Take it down. Clear the walls a bit. People like to imagine that *they* could be living in your house. They don't want to see *your* stuff around. They want to see room for *their* stuff. A house can't have too much personality, you know. Otherwise people can't feel like it could reflect their personality. Unless we find someone with exactly the same personality as yours . . ."

So much is communicated in the trailing off of a sentence. She is looking at me as though I were the lost needle that fell out of the haystack. It is clear she isn't counting on finding more like me.

"You never hung curtains? Your floors are beautiful. Have you got a big closet where we could hide some of these carpets?"

I am getting skittish. Maybe my sister would buy my house. Maybe I could just give it to her. She could pay my taxes. I'm wondering how to get rid of the realtor, and she's wondering how to get rid of me. I can tell.

"We'll have to have an open house. Just one day. Right away. That ought to do it. *If* you handle this properly. We'll invite realtors in the morning, and have the house open to visitors all afternoon. Everyone in town will want to see this house. It's been hidden away for so long."

Got it: single, unemployed, not dating, reading too much, drinking alone, reclusive. Still stung by the comment about curtains, I explain that I didn't need them because of those enormous ancient azaleas she wanted cut down—

"Not down. Back."

—and the house is so well protected from the street by all the trees, really eco-friendly, which is very hot these days, you know, I mean, the house is never hot, there is no need for air-conditioning—

"Yes, there is a lot of shade here. We'll have to turn on every light in the house. Where are the circuit breakers?"

I am stricken and pale by the end of our house tour. Somewhere deep inside my addled brain, I half expected her to turn to me and say, I love it, *I'll* buy it, and that would be the end of that. Maybe houses are like children. You can only see yours through eyes of love. Soon strangers will be tromping through my house, passing judgment on my taste, even though I'll have hidden it away so that they can feel at home. It's perverse. The only way to have an open house is to shut down everything that has made it your home.

"Don't worry. You don't have to be here. You don't have to be in town, even. I'll handle everything. Don't forget! Counters! Walls! Personality! Cleared!" She smiles graciously.

The following week, she sends over one of her associates to prod me down the open-house path to anonymous, sellable living.

I begin the Open House Project by taking everything personal off the walls—the children's paintings, the award certificates, the newspaper clippings. Time to wipe off the scribbles near the phone from when someone couldn't find a scrap of paper. As I am scrubbing, I'm thinking, Why bother? The new owners (I pray there will be new owners, and that they, too, will cherish my house) will simply paint over every sign of our history. I remember looking at old houses with a realtor many years ago, and seeing the intricate, penciled notations on a closet door marking the growth of two generations of children. At the time, I wondered why the owners hadn't cleaned things up for the sale; the sight of that door had made me feel like an intruder. But now I can appreciate the sheer impossibility of taking an eraser to the past.

The problem is simple: I am in love with my house. I found it. I'm the one who, as a young wife and mother, recognized its potential under the layers of eccentric neglect. I directed its resurrection and the renovation. I bought it again when our marriage faltered. I battled my way out of the depression that settled over me after the divorce by slowly bringing my house back to gracious, hospitable life. I have spent years basking in the beatitude of this home.

I have to admit that the house has taken on a lifelike quality, with its humming and grinding and grumbling noises, the walls like scrolls of shared history, proudly displaying each one of our achievements. The house, like any old thing, is needy, always breaking down or rotting and squeaking out for a patch of plaster or a slap of paint. I've taken care of it: twenty-five years of calling plumbers, electricians, carpenters, painters, garage door repairmen. Twenty-five years of trying to understand what they were talking about—sump pumps? Furnaces? Gutters? Twenty-five years of battling termites, moths, ants, spiders, skunks, crows, raccoons, and death's attendant maggots. Twenty-five years of collecting Helpful Men (those who know what to do about everything, and whose names I vow to pass on to the next owner). But it isn't in the structure of the house that the life seems to be leaching out; everything in the basement still grumbles and shudders. It is its soul that is slipping away. I had come to sense the spirit of the place as a real, recognizable, and familiar presence in my life, one that greeted me when I had been away, one that complained when I neglected it. Now I feel as if I were in the presence of a dying beast.

I have come to believe deeply that my house has protected me, even comforted me, and taken into its generous embrace, without question, the night's anguish and the night's joy. My house has known me, understood me, and soothed me. If Wendy and her brothers can have a big dog for a governess before they flee to Neverland, well, this house can be my Nana. Yet I am abandoning it. I am not too proud to tell you that every once in a while, as I pause in the doorway of a room, I lean into a wall and kiss it. I love my house, physically.

Such times are made for what my friend Jim calls the sound tracks of life.

"Try my *Songs of Sweet Sadness*," he says, when I tell him

about the Open House Project and accidentally confess that I've been kissing the walls. "It's a list of good, sad music I've put together over the years. I'll choose the perfect song for you."

One minute into Sarah McLachlan's "I Will Remember You" and I'm ready to start hugging the furniture. "Don't let your life pass you by/Weep not for the memories." I get Jim on the phone to beg for more.

"Yep," says Jim. "McLachlan wrote my anthem: 'Angel.' And do you know Patty Griffin? 'When It Don't Come Easy.' That's my theme song. And the song I want played at my funeral is Cat Power doing Dylan's 'Paths of Victory.' I've got the whole playlist in my iPod. Should I just send it?"

I'm not ready to plan my funeral, but I have to admire a man so deeply in touch with his inner girl.

My sons, however, want nothing to do with inner girls. They aren't at all indulgent or sympathetic. "Time to move on, Mom" seems to be the message. I call Alex, who can be counted on for a bracing tonic to my sentimental moods. As I talk to him, I walk from room to room.

"Alex, how can I give this house up? I'm walking around thinking this house has become The Museum of My Happiest Moments. I'm sure I'm making a big mistake. Don't you think? Maybe I can think of a way to stay. The Museum of My Happiest Moments—"

Alex is used to me by now.

"Time to build a new museum, Mom."

I call Theo at school in California and ask if he would like to get home before the open house, so that he can help me to decide what to pack and what to throw out. I have a fantasy of sharing tender, nostalgic memories with my baby.

"No, Mom," he replies. "I told you. I'm not attached to material things. They aren't what's important in life. Attachment causes suffering. Go ahead, do whatever you want. You have to learn to let go, Mom. Material things, they aren't real. Remember?"

Groovy, I feel like saying. Have I not spent plenty of real dollars on planks of wood with wheels attached to them, and pieces of plastic with knobs and cranks on them? It seems he is still reading a lot of Buddhist philosophy. A couple of days later I call him back and mention my plan to give away all the stuffed animals that have been sitting on an armchair in his bedroom for the past sixteen years, minding their own business. I can still remember exactly who gave him what; I can see my friend Byron walking in the kitchen door carrying the bunny; I can remember the enchanting store with the tree trunk full of stuffed animals running through the middle of it, in which we found the snake; I can remember when Theo was attached to the bear, and when the bear gave way to the dog, and when the dog, beaten down, conceded his place in Theo's bed to the cat. I make the phone call with a catch in my throat, looking over his menagerie.

"Don't touch my stuff, Mom," he says, panic rising in his voice. "I'm making a plane reservation as soon as we hang up. What's your credit card number again?"

*

The open house opens, and closes again. The realtor is upbeat.

"It was terrific! Perfect! Record turnout. People love your house. Don't worry, everything will work out!"

That realtor certainly knows how to turn on the lights. But she is right. Within a month the house has sold—to the young woman who lives across the street, and who has been admiring my garden through every season for years. In a weird twist of fate, she even has a toddler named Theodore.

Not a day goes by that I don't question my decision to sell. And not a day goes by that I don't thank my lucky stars that the house has sold. I have to admit that the minute my neighbor signs the contract, a huge wave of relief washes over me at the prospect of never again having to worry about the sump pump, the furnace, the shingles, or the wisteria. There is something liberating about lightening up the load of stuff I'm attached to. I'm actually enjoying those cleared counters.

There is no turning back. But in the last few months that the house is mine, I'm looking further and further back, into the days when I was pregnant with Theo, the days I lived here with my husband, the days when we arrived here with two-year-old Alex, back and back and back it goes as I wander from room to room. There's the Cold Room (we never could get the heat to work) full of skateboards and games and trunks of Legos. There's the room Alex annexed as an office for his homework.

There are a few bits of string dangling from the doorjamb, left over from the evening years ago when I came home from work to find Theo sitting on the floor outside Alex's office, as he insisted on calling the tiny attic room that held his desk. Alex was in his last month of high school, already eager to go to college, while Theo and I were contemplating four years of life together, just the two of us, missing Alex. We already felt abandoned. This whole process of children leaving home seems to go on forever; perhaps it starts when they take their first steps.

Theo was leaning against the wall, looking exhausted. He had laced most of what had been a huge ball of string from the light fixture in the hallway to each balcony railing to all the doorknobs, and then wedged it into the hinges of the door to Alex's room. He had taped it in several places to the floor and added a few more strands to the door molding and the ceiling for good measure. By the time he was done, he had strung hundreds of lines across the door. He had woven a giant, elaborate web of string. When I came upon this scene, Alex was sitting beyond the web, at his desk, doing his homework. He smiled ruefully and rolled his eyes when I waved at him from the hallway. I didn't even have to ask Theo what this was all about; he had trapped his brother in his office. I sat down beside him on the floor, put my arm around my little spider, and for a while we both watched Alex calmly continue to write his paper.

With the contract for the sale signed, I must face facts. Snow is pouring down from the sky as I sit in lonely silence in front of the fireplace, staring into the flames. I'm down to the last logs; what's the point of replenishing the woodpile? I will soon be moving. I decide to tackle culling the books, which brings on the biggest house crisis of all. Somehow, the anxiety I have—not only about moving, but more significantly, about growing old—ends up being concentrated on my books. I'm fairly certain that the next occupant of this house will be taking away bookshelves, beginning with the ones in the laundry room. I measure how many linear feet of books I have, just to get an idea of the magnitude of packing. I am confronted with the shocking revelation that I will never again own a house big enough for all my books. Every time I've gotten rid of a book in the past I've regretted it; two days after giving it away, I'll suddenly need the volume I hadn't glanced at in ten years, and I'll reach for the spot on the shelf it long occupied. I am bereft before I even begin sorting, and put the job off almost as soon as I start it.

I wander into the wine-colored library tucked under the staircase for the thousandth time, to see if I can make my books move by staring at them hard enough. I remember reading one afternoon during one of my off-again spells with Stroller; I was curled up on the small sofa under the window, nibbling my way through a box of my favorite After Eight chocolates, deep into Donald Hall's poem cycle about his wife's cancer. I was sobbing about as hard as was possible while still being able to see straight. I read about Jane Kenyon's dying, Donald Hall's anguish, his sense of utter hopelessness—and his abiding love for her. I read about how he nursed her, how constant his attention was, how tender his hands, and how poignant her sense of impending departure. Who would keen for me that way, as only a lover can, if cancer ever came to carry me away?

Alex had walked into the room and taken a long look at me, crying on the couch.

"Mom, what's the point? Just stop. Stop reading. Put the book down."

That's always been my problem. I just can't close the book, no matter how much it makes me cry. I am under a spell, hoping that all will end well, even when it clearly isn't going to.

But now, wandering through my home, saying goodbye, knowing I'm coming to the end of a chapter, I fully appreciate how much magic I've been living in all along. It isn't the end of the tale that counts. It's the story—it's being *in* the story.

My son is right: time for that new Museum of Happiest Moments.

7. THE SHADOWS COME INTO PLAY

I T TAKES A while for the finality of the sale to sink into my resistant brain, but it does, and once I accept that someone else will soon be living in my house, I start digging into closets, rooting through my stuff to figure out what I'm carrying into my next life. I start in the kitchen, and oddly, for someone who doesn't cook, I stay there for hours on end. I never fully realized how central to my life that room has become until I begin to dismantle it. It certainly isn't because of all the dreamy meals I whipped up in there. I can count on one hand the number of dinner parties I've thrown over the last ten years.

Some of the drawers are crammed with cracked and rusted items, sifters whose handles are stuck and nonstick pans whose glazes are peeling off. It is time to throw them away. But other shelves are piled with snowy tablecloths (in pristine condition) and flower vases (which my sister will want) and, best of all, shelf after shelf of cookbooks (which my sister will also want). Many of them are still shrink-wrapped. My kitchen was never about cooking; it simply became my living room—the room in which I hung out with my children, and with Stroller whenever he came around. The living room, oddly, became the place where I spent quiet time alone, where I read, or stared into the fire, or played my piano. I think two things largely contributed to the kitchen's appeal: the cradling sofa, and the most important—and underrated—piece of kitchen equipment, the radio.

I first learned about radios from Stroller, whose furnishing rule of thumb was to have a radio in every room. He did this for the ball games, mainly, and God knows I wasn't the first woman to fall asleep in his bed to the sound of the Yankees going a few extra innings on a summer night. It was blissful. I'm woefully undereducated when it comes to baseball, but I am happy to be told what's going on. In fact, whenever Stroller wanted my company at a game at Yankee Stadium, he always plugged earbuds into my head, stuffed a pocket radio tuned to the game into my coat, and put a hot dog in my fist. This way, I could follow what was going on in front of me and thoroughly enjoy myself. I could even sound smart, stealthily throwing out an observation that had just been slipped into my head, like a newscaster with a prompter. I got so good at aping the announcer that occasionally Stroller, who could fathom neither the depths of my ignorance nor my groveling desire to be a good student, would look severely—and hopefully—at me, eyebrow arched, and ask if it was me talking, or the radio.

Not that ball games necessarily brought out the best in Stroller, as I learned when he invited me on a very special trip to Fenway Park for a Yankees vs. Red Sox game. I was flattered by his faith in my newly developed discernment, until I realized he really just wanted me to do the driving. When we got to the stadium, Stroller deposited me in my seat somewhere far away in the bleachers, plugged me into the radio, found the proper station broadcasting the game, and then left. He settled himself next to an old friend somewhere behind home plate. He was so far away that I couldn't even see where he was. I know this is one of those fine points of etiquette that would leave most guys scratching their heads, wondering what the problem was. After all, it was impossible to get tickets; Stroller had to find a scalper for mine. What was he supposed to do, give up his prime seat on his friend's season ticket? Now, that would be unreasonable. What did I know about baseball?

I thought the chauffeur deserved a bit better, but I settled in quickly. My neighbors began brawling with one another before the game started, and midway through the first inning rivulets of beer were pooling at my feet. A couple of fans screamed excitedly in Japanese into their cell phones every time Hideki Matsui came into view, and they narrated the entire game to fans back home. In the end, I had a great time—because of the radio, and also because an enormous fracas between some of the players broke out in the pen below me, and while everyone else was craning their necks for a view of this exciting development, I had a front-row seat and got to be on TV.

Listening to games on the radio at home was a different matter. Not having the visuals when you're a novice is a challenge. Instead of following the action, I became entranced by the symphonic quality of the sounds of a game coming over the radio: the crescendos of the crowd roaring when something exciting happened, the dissonant chords when the umpire was a blockhead, the thematic quality of most of the calls, the digressions at quieter intervals. Best of all was the counterpoint of Stroller's rapid-fire commentary with that of the announcer; it was like a baseball concerto, and it washed over me in a bath of shared pleasure.

Stroller always said baseball was the most interesting game of all, because as in life, his theory went, anything is possible at any moment, but unlike life, baseball isn't played against time. Each moment is filled with infinite possibility. No two games are ever the same. Well, the fact that he didn't consider life to be exactly like baseball in these regards might have been problematic. I've never been in a position to argue about baseball, though to my naïve way of thinking, it seems that any game involving men tossing things around—no, make that any game involving men, period—could never be predictable. However, Stroller did introduce me to the one great concept that has become the dominant theme of this period of my life.

Late one afternoon we were listening to a broadcast from Yankee Stadium. By then we had settled into a rhythm of weekends at his house in the country, as Stroller did not want to spend time at my house. I was lying low, trying to maintain a tranquil, undemanding, small happiness. I was still knitting the blueberry-colored scarf I had started and abandoned years earlier, to wrap around Stroller's neck. When I returned to it, I must have picked up my needles the wrong way, and with the twist in the yarn and the change in direction, I knit a vivid scar right into stitches, which seemed appropriate, given what had been going on. The radio announcer began describing the influence of the setting sun—between home plate and first base—on the game.

"The pitcher's mound is bathed in light, and home plate is lost in patches of shade," he said. "The players are having difficulty picking up balls going from sunlight to shade."

I thought the announcer was being charmingly poetic.

"The shadows come into play," continued the announcer, drawing out the words with great portent.

The shadows come into play. I repeated it a few times, enthralled by the beauty of such a phrase coming from so unlikely a source. What a useful concept, I remarked to Stroller, at this time in our lives. How hard it can be to keep an eye on what's important, not be distracted by confusing patterns. Better to get out of the shadows . . .

Stroller set me straight at once.

"And the shadows will be in play for a while," Stroller added, with a peculiar emphasis. "Yankee Stadium has a particularly high perimeter wall."

I might have guessed.

Baseball games aren't usually the best broadcasts for cooking or dining, whether you are with someone or alone, as they are too distracting, and if the Yankees are botching things, too upsetting. But the great thing about a radio is that you can listen to anything you like, and no one has a lock on the dial. It is easy to change the station. Stroller's favorite stations for cooking played old-time dance music from the 1940s and '50s, which always makes me think of my aunt Kathleen. She taught me to dance. She, my father, sisters, brother, and I would dance arm in arm, cheek to cheek, hip to hip, waltzing, fox-trotting, twisting, gliding, and gyrating our way across the tiled floor of the family room. When Kathleen spoke of my father, "L. D." (Louis DeLoach Browning), he seemed a different, mysterious person. As teenagers in Kentucky, she and he had won county prizes for Best Charleston and Best Fox-Trot.

Nowadays, Kathleen lives in what used to be called a nursing home, but given the shows, the dining, the dances, the lectures, and the field trips, I'm more inclined to call it an elder hostel, with the inevitable turnover of people checking in and out. Kathleen had a hard time adjusting to the place. Imagine having to pack up the house you've lived in for sixty years, and winnowing your things to fit into one room. Now imagine that you have never before thrown anything away, ever, for sixty years. This will give you an inkling of the job Kathleen had moving into her rest-of-her-life room. For months we got phone calls from our cousins: "Does anyone want the enormous old mahogany bed that used to belong to our great-great-grandmother? What about a few more quilts?"

At least she had family to help her. Moving house turned out to be a big topic of conversation among Kathleen's new friends at the nursing home. Mobility, specifically, was the issue. Pain in every joint. One of them had solved the difficulty of having to climb stairs to pack up her large house by throwing the contents of drawers out the window from the second floor and letting the neighbors take what they wanted off the lawn. Another man, foreseeing the pain of creaking knees, had emptied his second and third floors years earlier, and set up camp on the ground floor, turning the dining room into the bedroom so he could be near the kitchen. When I asked my father whether there was anything at all good about getting old, he replied, "Yes, being alive."

Kathleen had lived energetically. She taught my sisters and me how to twist when we were little girls. She taught us every move she knew. My father always found the music irresistible, and he would join us, grabbing our hands, throwing us under him, across his arms, Kathleen in her swishy skirt, we girls in our freshly ironed pajamas, all of us doing the boogie-woogie across the floor, every move we could—crisscrossing arms and knees, springing from partner to partner, twisting on one heel, way down low to the floor, shoulders dipping and swooping. When the music got hot, Kathleen would hoot and holler.

"Faster, girls! Faster!"

We twisted our little hips as fast as they could go.

Kathleen also taught us all the words to the melancholy love songs she loved so much, and years later, when my babies were little, I sang them as lullabies—"Sentimental Journey," "Bye Bye Blackbird," "Swing Low, Sweet Chariot"—until one night Theo begged me to stop because it was all so sad.

I can't hear dance music without hearing Kathleen's voice, and many's the time I've taken myself for a spin, having learned the old broom-as-partner trick long ago, probably from Fred Astaire. Stroller and I loved dancing in the kitchen; we would push aside the table and chairs to clear space, and he would sweep me into a waltz or a fox-trot. He asked me to teach him some basic boogie-woogie on the piano, which he repeated endlessly, with raucous conviction. We had such a good time dancing in the kitchen that we decided to take dancing lessons.

Big mistake. It turned out we were both doing many things wrong with our waltzes and fox-trots. The teacher began to take the steps apart and show us the proper patterns. Suddenly we couldn't enjoy dancing together. Where I had once adjusted to the quirks of his rhythms, I now understood that they were mistakes, and, good student that I had always been, I wanted to do things properly. Stroller would ask me to count the beats, but this was infuriating for both of us because it made me seem bossy. "But I'm not the one who told you what was wrong!" I would wail. In the middle of a song, Stroller would abruptly stop in frustration at having lost the beat or tangled up our feet, and then would be angry at me for trying to get us back on track. "Why do you always have to lead?" he would say. He had grown up taking dancing lessons in twee classes, the girls wearing white gloves, with his nose stuffed into the teacher's cleavage. I had grown up dancing with my little sister in my arms, and she had to be led. I pointed out to Stroller that I had never had a problem being led by my father, who had a meticulous, smooth, yet insouciant style—but when you are dancing, the last thing you want to do is hurl Freud at one another.

Our teacher would try to guide us with marvelously profound and unhelpful comments: "Stroller! You must signal to her that you want to execute a spin. You must signal that you are changing direction. No! No! Your signals must be subtle.

You don't need to push her. Just a light pressure in the small of the back."

The problem was that I had become used to being hurled around by Stroller, and rather liked the force-of-nature feel to our stomps. I had liked dancing when I hadn't been worried about doing it the right way, and so had he.

"Dancing is about two people in balance," our teacher would say. "You have to do two things at the same time: you have to find balance as a couple, and you each have to find your own individual balance. Each of you has to maintain your center. Stroller, if you hold her too close, she has no room to maneuver. She can't keep her balance. But you can't move so far back, either. Then there is no more couple."

Well, it didn't get any simpler than that. We gave up on the lessons.

The radio in the kitchen is terrific for quieter evenings, too. You can stumble on composers you've never heard before, and, these days, language you've never heard before too. The radio is perfect company: easy on the ear, quick to change the subject, demanding nothing in response, not even your attention. It doesn't ask you to make any decisions. It doesn't ask for any maintenance. It just gives and gives, singing or talking its heart out. As I said, the best, and cheapest, appliance in the kitchen.

It has occurred to me to wonder if the kitchen is so seductive precisely because I didn't cook all that often. I mean, if I had to whip up breakfast, lunch, and dinner seven days a week, all year round, perhaps it wouldn't be so thrilling to have someone come around, pat my behind, snuffle around the pots, and ask me when dinner will be ready. That means there is something to be said for treating a hot meal as a *novelty item*. I still think aprons—the old-fashioned kind, made of pretty cotton prints, with wide skirts and pockets and ties—are very alluring.

Of course, if you are in the kitchen with your lover, you want to be making the sort of thing that doesn't require too much concentration, what with the dancing and the ball games and all. This is where crabmeat comes in; there are an infinite number of ways to toss crabmeat into other ingredients, and then nestle it into the hollow of an avocado, or amid a fan of grapefruit, and present a plate with bravado. Lobster salad has the same quality. Basically, any food that someone else has done all the hard work of preparing fits the bill. You do, after all, want to exit the kitchen with some semblance of dignity, leaving some impression, however vague, that you will be able not only to find, but also to follow the path of the stomach to the fellow's heart. I suppose, speaking as a feminist, I should add that he ought to be able to do the same for you; however, we have seen where that leads. Competitive cooking. It is more fun, in my book, for a home-cooked meal to be a novelty item all the way around. Let takeout carry the burden of banality.

The kitchen can be a very romantic place. Of course, if you're with the right person, the driveway can be a romantic place, too. But the kitchen, with the refrigerator and the radio humming, and everything ranged tidily on the shelves, offering a feeling of order and sustenance, is certainly a good place to get memories spinning. I have logged many hours in the kitchen so wrapped in thought that my head might as well have been on backwards; I could have sworn that the recipe I had been staring at for ten minutes called for a teaspoon of suffering when all it said was salt. I once asked my aunt Kathleen—who will tell you that at least in the nursing home, she is liberated from the stove—if she spent a lot of her time now looking back on the past.

"Honey," she said, "that's not the direction I'm going in."

Still, I have to keep reminding myself, wistfulness should not be my favorite ingredient in the kitchen. That would be allspice.

8. LEFTOVERS

M Y UNEMPLOYMENT "FEED ME" vibes seem to have brought a couple of men out of the woodwork. Perhaps some like a rescue mission when they see one. Or maybe it's simply that some men are less intimidated by a woman who isn't a player in the work world. In any case, I now am seen as more available. I haven't been turning down any invitations to dine, no matter how blind the date. Even I have had to face facts: you can only eat so many cookies. A good meal will always get me out of bed. It never occurs to me that it might be supposed to get me *into* bed.

Anyway, once you are unemployed, people think there's no longer any excuse for you to be single, as you must have all the time in the world to focus on this thorny issue. The pressure becomes weirdly intense. I am constantly being asked if I've met anyone yet. It seems like everyone is developing rescue strategies for me. I could go to the dry cleaner and my sister would want to know if there were any cute guys there. No one seems to understand how much time it takes to actually find work. Between that and falling apart, I've got my hands full. Even my mother besieges me: "Make an effort! Put something on your face!"

It is on one of these early unemployment dates that I am told that I eat like a horse. I consider this a compliment. Many single women have dating horror stories, I'm sure. I don't. I'm basically of the Greyhound Bus School of Blind Dates: I consider myself a tourist on a short trip. With a round-trip ticket.

There are two rules of thumb for successful blind dating. The first involves developing the art of paying attention. You will not be wasting your time, as this talent is as useful at a conference table as it is at a dinner table. A man will tell you (or show you) everything you need to know about him within the first fifteen minutes of your meeting, which is why I like to keep my mouth shut and just listen, eat, and drink. Think about it: The guy who has no table manners. The guy who hasn't spoken to his mother in twenty years. The one who never sees his kids. The guy who hates his job—and has hated the last three he's had in the past decade. The guy whose favorite job was converting people to his Pentecostal faith—that's the one where you speak in tongues. The guy who would feel more relaxed knowing if you'll go to bed with him when dinner is over, so would you mind letting him know before the appetizer is served? (I kid you not.) The guy whose wife has just—he is heartbroken to tell you—been diagnosed with cerebral palsy, and there is only so much pain a guy can bear. But hey, the drugs these days are amazing! You can't even tell she's sick! The guy who tells you he's kept his driver waiting, as he's on his way to his private plane for a trip to Rome.

"Business?"

"No! Funsy!"

Yes, there are guys who still talk this way. But a girl's got to eat.

Let's not even go into that strangely proliferating breed, the guy who has been in a sad marriage for years—but remains married to his wife, with whom he has "an understanding." Of course, he's the only one with that understanding. How did he get on your dance card? Meanwhile, you're riffling through your mental Rolodex, wondering who exactly this guy would be good for, and what the hell your friend was thinking when she said you'd be perfect for each other.

Of course, you can listen as hard as you want, and you still won't hear everything. Stroller neglected to mention one of his wives when he first related his life count to me, and it was only months later that a friend of mine chanced to hear about wife number three (actually number one) at a party. Naturally, I heatedly told my friend she must have misheard, only to learn from a slightly sheepish Stroller that he had, indeed, fudged the numbers.

Admittedly, we are, at my age, in the "leftover years." We're all left over from one failed relationship or another. That's fine—it just takes getting used to. These are the years when "Don't ask, don't tell" makes a lot of sense. It is not, for example, a good idea to ask what happened to the previous wife, or, more often, wives; that is classified as more than you need to know on a first date, though that won't stop many men from telling you. The kids have a new term for this: oversharing. There is no need to know why he dumped her (or vice versa), unless you want a hint of why he will dump you (or vice versa). If you read the end of the book first, you'll lose interest in the beginning.

Recently, I was shown to the table that my blind date (why don't we just call him a stranger?), apparently a regular customer at this restaurant, normally reserved for interviews. And by the way, many men have this stuff down to a science, complete with secret signals for the maître d' about how fast or slow the service should be. I know this because one man broke the code of brotherhood and told me about it. Anyway, on this particular evening I was kept waiting for about half an hour; my date was violating the twenty-minute rule, but he did call to say he was stuck in traffic. Plus, it was an excellent restaurant, and I was very hungry. I finally ordered a glass of a light, sparkling white wine to bide my time, and had taken just a few sips when the powerhouse arrived. Glancing at my drink, he waved the waiter over, had him remove it, and asked him to pour two goblets of a rich red Bordeaux that he had had the foresight to bring with him. He had two bottles, actually, but he quickly sized me up as a one bottle event. Of course it is generous and thoughtful of someone to bring wine to share with a stranger at a restaurant. It shows foresight and planning.

Or is it controlling? Did anyone even ask what I wanted to drink? Or notice that I was already drinking it?

In any sociological study of the dating game, the billionaire is an intriguing cohort. Quite apart from a fascinating display of nouveau entitlement, he comes with a sort of added attraction in the behavior he draws out of those around him. My favorite billionaire moment involved watching not one, not two, but three women slip past our table in a somber, dim restaurant, brushing my date's elbow, leaving behind a discreet card. The guy shrugged as he pocketed them. This happened all the time.

I never mind waiting for a date to show up, as it gives me much-needed practice eating alone in restaurants, which terrifies me. Some of my friends are masters of this art. One has strict rules of etiquette: you can read a newspaper or a magazine during your meal, but not a book. A book sends the message that you do this all the time (particularly if you are on page 380 of *Anna Karenina*); a periodical says this was a spur-of-the-moment impulse. You can read during breakfast and lunch, my friend explains, but never at dinner. It is simply not appropriate. She would never deny herself the pleasure of eating alone. What would she do if she got a hankering for Indian food, for instance? Or Ethiopian? Cook it for herself? Besides, dining alone gives her a chance to indulge in one of her worst habits when dining with others: eavesdropping.

It is perfectly bad manners to act like you are dining alone while you are dining with someone else, even if it is your husband, worse if it is your lover. However, it is also irresistible. How can you possibly avoid checking every other table in the room once you sit down? You never know what you might find. Why, I was once mesmerized through dinner by a beautiful woman at the next table; she was in her thirties, dressed in designer clothing, and sucked her thumb through the entire meal. First I thought she was just licking something off her fingers, but no. She took a bite of food, joined the conversation with her boyfriend and another couple for a moment, and then leaned back in her armchair, and, with a loud sigh of contentment, resumed sucking her thumb. Every once in a while she gave it a rest, releasing it from her mouth, letting it hover in front of her face, her fingers still curled loosely, the wrinkled, glistening thing just tipped off her lips. Her boyfriend leaned over and nuzzled her sweetly. I, of course, missed the entire conversation at my table, as it was all I could do to keep from walking over to find out everything about someone so uninhibited that she could regress in public.

One does get into bad habits. I am an inveterate eavesdropper. I have even worked hard to develop a weird ability to hear two conversations at once, one in each ear, though I haven't yet learned to make sense of either. It is far better to concentrate on simple eavesdropping. I have a very active fantasy life, so I am constitutionally incapable of seeing people at a meal and not spinning theories about who they are, where they work, and why they are truly miserable even though they look happy. I find this entertaining. My sons find it embarrassing. I reminded them that their own very beloved grandmother did the same thing, specializing in the creation of complex family pathologies of complete strangers related to her only by their proximity to her table. I am simply following in her footsteps, but that doesn't alleviate my children's mortification.

Alex has developed a neat trick to get my attention when it has wandered too far away from our table. He puts his fist up to his mouth and makes loud, choking, wire-shorting noises as though he has a walkie-talkie. "*Cccccrackle crackle crackle*. Come in, Mom. Dinner in progress. Come in, Mom. *Crackle crackle crackle. Ccccc*. Do you read me?" As my hearing gets worse, I have to work harder to catch other people's conversations in loud rooms, which, come to think of it, is a very good reason to dine alone. I don't know why I think people at other tables are more interesting than those at mine—I have no idea who they are, but of course that explains it; something along the lines of familiarity breeding contempt, though surely not that bad. I might also add that it reveals an unusually happy, optimistic streak in my nature to believe in the high quality of conversational life all around me.

You never know when you might learn something valuable from a stranger's conversation. But you know exactly what you are going to learn from the conversation at your table, because you have had the same conversation many, many times. If your companions complain about your eavesdropping, and invariably they do, you might suggest, gently but firmly, that they continue talking, because you can guarantee that someone at the next table is hanging on their every word. Everyone eavesdrops.

By the way, if you happen upon one of those charmed moments when you are lucky enough to know who is being filleted by the diners at the next table, you have only two options before you: either inform your neighbors immediately that you are friends with the subject of their dinner conversation, so they have the option of changing the topic, or remain silent forever. The worst thing to do is to listen to the entire conversation, and, as you are paying the bill, announce to your neighbors that they are wrong about your best friend. But it is an awfully tempting course. Just be forewarned that this will place you in a moral gray area. Unless, of course, you are the subject of conversation at the next table, in which case all is fair, and I suggest inflicting maximum shock and awe.

I was very careful never to risk such bad behavior with Stroller, who monitored my attention (to him) levels carefully. He had a jealous streak. One evening during a large dinner party, I was engrossed in conversation, as is the custom of the country, with the fellow to my left, when suddenly I felt my chair, with me in it, sliding across the floor. Stroller had hooked his foot around a rung and was pulling me closer to him. When I complained about his possessiveness to a friend, she shrieked in dismay at my stupidity. "Are you kidding? That bothers you? I would give anything for my husband to be jealous of me."

For a long time, I thought one of the most depressing things to watch was a couple dining together and not talking. This happens all the time, no matter how fancy the restaurant. I used to think it only happened with elderly couples, but I notice more middle-aged couples giving each other the silent treatment at the dinner table these days. I also used to think this was sad, shocking, and even abusive. Why didn't they just go ahead and kill each other, or at least get divorced? However, now that I have become a much less judgmental single person, I have decided that it is very generous of each person to give the other the kind of silence we all crave from time to time, the kind of silence in which you can really savor your meal, and listen in on other people's table talk. After all, you can listen to your partner on the way home—and think of all the new observations you'll have to share!

The truly depressing thing these days is the number of people at the same table who are deep in conversation on their cell phones. It is a chronic symptom of our overconnected, underengaged times, a way of being neither here nor there, and certainly not in the moment. Texting has even become more compelling than talking—let alone listening. But the addiction creeps over us silently and stealthily. One of the side effects of unemployment, for me, was such a sag in self-esteem that the antidote was to feel constantly needed, and to judge that by the ringing phone. I had to start forcing myself to leave the cell phone home when I went out.

Eating alone at home is another matter entirely. Eating however you want is the pinnacle of release, especially if you are unremittingly judgmental about other peoples' bad table manners. Go ahead, hold that cold slab of leftover steak in your fist and tear into it. You are a lioness. Eat whenever you want—nothing wrong with whipping up a batch of popovers at 2 A.M. Eat whatever you want—nothing wrong with peanut butter and bananas for breakfast. Eat wherever you want—gnaw on salami while deadheading the roses; shovel in the pasta while standing at the sink, to save yourself the trip with the dirty dish. However, I do recommend that you finish chewing before you start running the water.

When you are a single parent, dating, you have to confront the matter of how and when to include children at the table. I was a failure on this front. I only once brought my children on a date with me, as we were all invited for lunch. I didn't know this fellow all that well, but he, too, lived in the suburbs and had children, so we thought, Why not? I arrived to find that in his neighborhood the houses were enormous, maintained by household staffs, and surrounded by horse pastures—with horses in them. Somewhere a rooster was crowing. The table in my date's kitchen was beautifully set; clearly we were to eat alone, while the children were led to a trough somewhere. There was a fully uniformed cook at the stove; I was anticipating a gourmet lunch. A servant ladled soup into our bowls, and darned if it didn't look familiar, all those slippery noodles floating on top of a greasy broth. My suspicions were confirmed with a glance at the cans on the kitchen counter, though I'd recognize the taste anywhere: Campbell's Chicken Noodle Soup.

In the meantime, outside, halfway through our tuna sandwiches, we heard a ruckus coming from a pasture. My date's teenagers had loaded my children into the open bed of a pickup truck and driven them over to a colony of beehives standing at the back of a meadow. While the teens honked the horn wildly and nosed up as close as they could get to the boxes without knocking them over, stirring up swarms of angry bees, my children cowered in fetal positions in the back, hands over their heads, screaming and sobbing.

Lunch was over.

I had custody of my boys half of every week. When they were at my house, I wanted to give them my full attention, so I split my life in two: boy nights and man nights. Each good practice for the other, I might add. I believe this is what is known in the trade as compartmentalization, and after all these years I am a pro. I just didn't want them to feel they had any competition for my attention—the boys, that is.

I hardly ever invited a man home to join us at our table. The couple of times I did, in the course of fifteen years since getting divorced, were not exactly what I would call successes. My first guest was a gentleman of the old school, so old that, even though he had lived in Manhattan his entire life, he had never visited a suburb of New York. He spent quite a bit of time bragging about this at dinner.

"Where on earth are we?" he kept asking the boys. "What is this place?"

The children were aghast. "You're at our house. We live here!"

"But I've driven right past this town a thousand times! It never existed!"

Two small, newly shampooed towheads swiveled around to glare at our guest. They could smell his snobbery, and it was not pleasant. They knew an insult when they heard one, even if they were wearing pajamas. As soon as dinner was over I conspicuously pulled the bright red train schedule out of my bag. I walked my annoying visitor to the station, a walk I had made every morning and every evening for years—but this was the last time he would make it. He grumbled about how "weird" everything was, sweeping his arm grandly across sidewalks and trees and houses glowing warmly in the dark, as if he were having an out-of-body experience on an alien planet. Out of my own old-school sense of propriety, I offered to wait for his train with him, but within moments I was overwhelmed with vivid, terrifying fantasies of pushing him off the platform into the oncoming train, sort of a reverse Anna Karenina move, and I had to leave. I did not need a therapist to explain my hostility. And neither did my children, who were glad to see him go.

My one other benighted dinner guest spent a great deal of time talking about his global travels, to the delight of Alex, who even at the age of twelve adored a plane trip, unlike his brother, who loathed leaving his bed. My guest began talking about a trip to Antarctica and invited me along to join him. In front of the children. The moment dinner was over and we said goodbye and closed the door, two snarling faces confronted me.

"He invited you to the South Pole?" said Theo. "That's really far! You can't go there!"

"And he didn't even invite us!" said Alex. "That's the worst part. He thinks he's taking you away? You think you're going without me? I'm the one who wants to see Antarctica. We hate him."

So much for a balanced melding of the personal and the more personal.

A few years later, when Stroller was in my life, I would beg him to join us for dinner, even offering to roast a chicken and make chocolate soufflé, but dinner with the boys was beyond his psychological ken. He considered it some form of entrapment, which, of course, it was. How could anyone, loving me, not love my children? I stopped asking him. (To be strictly fair, I note that in his deliberate way, Stroller did come to know my sons a bit, and helped one get a summer job.) Stroller's wife had made it clear that if he wanted to see his own kids, it would be on her terms—which did not include another woman. It didn't make any difference that their mess of a marriage long predated me. I was "the devil." I had not been allowed to meet their children, much less be in the same room with them. Nothing, you might say, had ever been well integrated.

Alas, one grows accustomed to the complications of (so-called) adult relationships.

Which leads me, finally, to the second rule of thumb for successful midlife dating: the refinement of a determinedly good attitude. You must bring yourself to believe that everyone, no matter how strange or boring he might be, has at least one interesting thing to tell you—whether it's the population of stoners in Hawaii in the '60s, the population of billionaires in Boise, Idaho, or the population of migratory swallows off the coast of Sardinia. (That last one, though, rated a close call with my trusty "Worth another meal?" assessment system. Migratory swallows? What kind of man would count such a thing? Sadly, one who lives in Italy.)

Are you thinking this is all sounding a tad cynical? Let me assure you that I have met some wonderful men on blind dates; I've had dinner with interesting, convivial, warm, accomplished men more than a few times. Some of my best friends are men. I love men; I've raised two of them. My point, though, if I were to take a management consultant perspective on dating, is that it isn't a highly effective way to spend time. The odds of casting a wide net and hauling in that special whale of a guy are pretty low, for all sorts of reasons, not the least of which is the fisherwoman's determinedly grumpy attitude—and the flimsiness of nets. When you get right down to it, I don't want to go out and find love. I want love to find me, magically, as it is supposed to. I want love to come the old-fashioned way, by accident. Not by harpoon. I don't want to feel like I'm going out on . . . job interviews.

The truth is, I have come to hate dating. I'm tired of having a good attitude. I've pretty much given up trying to tell my side of the story to most of my blind dates. It isn't worth the trouble of interrupting them to get their attention. Hence, I call these encounters jukebox dinners. You drop in a dime—starting things off with, say, a simple question, like, "How are you?"—and a couple of hours later the tunes are still playing, until suddenly your date will look over tenderly, lean into the table, and remark, "Say, you *are* a good listener. But enough about me. Tell me about yourself. Waiter, check please!"

This is fine with me. I get to order to my heart's content, eat like a horse, not worry about making a good impression, not worry about the price of beef that was marbleized in Japan, and I get to practice: practice my sage nod; practice my knowing glance; practice my sensitive smile; practice my impersonation of a psychiatrist—"Yes. Go on"; practice raising one eyebrow; switch to the other eyebrow; practice the stealthy moves involved in locating my lost shoe under the table without drawing any attention to the problem; practice left-handedness; practice the multiplication table, especially sevens.

Why bother, you wonder? Can't you practice holding your knife in your left hand at home, privately and comfortably? Of course not. When I am dining alone, I am comfortable, and private, and can focus on interesting, provocative things, like books. I'm on a blind date for one thing only. If I get lucky.

Leftovers.

9. BUILDING STANDARD

As the months go by, I'm increasingly unhappy that I'm spending so much time alone. Strangers at the dinner table do not count as good company. Now, I'm a feminist from way back. As a teenager I wore a T-shirt exclaiming: A WOMAN NEEDS A MAN LIKE A FISH NEEDS A BICYCLE. I pride myself on never having been dependent on a man after I left home. These days, maybe because I'm not working, my independent spirit has wilted. When I hear myself say, "If I fall in love again, fine; if I don't, that's great too," I don't believe it. I love being in love. I love it so much, in fact, that I am ready to convince myself that a relationship is worth any price, even if it costs me the compromising of some fundamental values. But what, exactly, are those values, at this point in my life? The answer isn't clear.

Well, unemployment is certainly giving me plenty of time to think things over. The busyness of work is gone. "At the back of that hurry is the knowledge that it is a screen against honesty," Adam Nicolson wrote in *Sea Room*. I recognize that feeling. I had often had it at the office.

Stroller handsomely surfaces, upon learning about the end of the magazine, with advice about crisis management—about which he knows a great deal, having managed the biggest crisis in my life until then: himself. He is well acquainted with my terror of unemployment, having heard enough about it over the years, and though he is in many ways completely irrational, in the ways of the world he is a realist. He doesn't mind if I cannot not get out of my heavy flannel nightgown when he visits, and I am beyond caring how I look. All I want is a blankie. I am feeling, in a large, dark corner of my soul, unemployable *and* unlovable, a lethal combination.

He takes it upon himself to talk me down off the financial ledge, even though I can hardly follow a word he's saying. I've had no trouble understanding the most complex financial stories in the newspapers, but when it comes to my own finances, I become dim-witted, picking at the lace on my sleeves, hugging my knees to my chest, and tenting myself under my nightgown. Stroller remains patient, as with a child. He jabs at my bank statements, and all I can see are parentheses. Losses. The market dropped so precipitously that my life savings are shrinking before my eyes—and I have to live off those. What is he talking about, tax write-offs? My ears begin booming, my eyes grow cloudy with tears, and my mind wanders.

Stroller generously offers to rent me an apartment he owns in New York City so that I can have a place to live near whatever future employment might arise. It is a beautiful apartment and would have been perfect for the two of us. But whenever I spend time there I become sad. Just walking through the door, I am flooded with yearning for what might have been, what could be. After all, it had seemed so within reach.

I am unable and unwilling to grasp, much less to accept, what is happening. In the present tense.

I am on my own.

And I am scared and lonely. Even my friends cannot fill this emptiness.

I keep second-guessing myself, as I have for years. Stroller would return to status quo ante in a minute, if I agreed to his terms. His invitations to join him for dinner become more alluring with every passing week. One doesn't want to fall back into a relationship with trouble for the wrong reasons, though admittedly, there are times when the wrong reasons are good ones. Well, perhaps we could build a friendship. (Again, another entrance ramp onto that highway of denial yawning open before me.)

Stroller is solicitous. Distance has made his heart kinder and more patient. And he needs the stubbornness of a mule with me, because I am constantly trying to change the subject from the stock market and tax issues, asking him why he can't just file for divorce and get on with life. I mean, he is already paying child support, alimony, you name it. This situation is even more confusing than my finances, but much more interesting and vexing. He sighs deeply, shrugs, and says, not unkindly, "I wish I knew. Why does it matter to you?" Whereupon it is my turn to shrug and sigh. It is amazing how adult conversations can regress to variations on the way we talk to children: *It matters because I said so.*

Why, you must be wondering by now, was I so attached to Stroller? Well, for starters, he liked to hold hands. That may sound trivial, but bear with me. That's one of my favorite things to do; it makes me feel safe and loved, and it reminds me of being a child, of being a mother, and of simply being connected to someone. And we had fun; Stroller made me laugh, and I delighted him. He understood me. He was spontaneously generous, creative, and thoughtful about special occasions and unusual treats. We enjoyed the same proportions of noisy engagement and quiet; we both needed solitude and valued independence. These qualities are not so readily found. Love isn't so easy to tumble into—except when it is.

I'm not the first person to splash around in the psycho-analytic ocean of reasons for bad relationships; there's nothing I'm handier at than revisiting old psychic wounds. But not everything can be reduced to neurosis, not even by me. Even if it could be, there isn't much point in going all the way back to the beginning. Love, as my own analyst said years ago, is complicated. Stroller was eccentric, no doubt, but I'm one of those people for whom eccentrics were made. I'm an appreciator of the offbeat. And, having been raised in a highly charged and rather eccentric household, I developed what you might call a very high tolerance for difficulty.

But I had no idea what I was up against.

Stroller takes to sending me e-mails about things like budgets. What is my household budget? What percentage of my income do I spend on electricity? I am dumbfounded. I have never answered to anyone about my spending. I have always lived within my means. I have no debt. Is this a peek at the way husbands talk to wives?

I get my answer when Stroller starts leaving me voice mails that are clearly not meant for me—he isn't drunk dialing, as the kids would say, but in some part of his brain he must be guilt dialing. "I've just written all the checks you requested. But you have to get the spending under control," he would say. "You can begin by turning off the lights when you leave the room."

At first I am confused by these messages, as Stroller isn't writing checks for me and I always turn off the lights, even when I'm in the room. Then one evening, while I am sitting contentedly in fresh pajamas, eating a box of graham crackers and reading yet another Patricia Cornwell novel, bones and blood on my mind, I pick up a message from Stroller saying he is running late, go ahead and order for him. That is when I finally understand that he thinks he is dialing his wife, and I am left to wonder how she knows what he would have for dinner, and how he knows she isn't turning off the lights.

All in all, it isn't looking like I am going to be able to build my new Museum of Happiest Memories in New York. It's time to leave.

Fourteen years earlier, after getting divorced, I had bought a house on the coast of Rhode Island, in a place where the only thing that comes between "Liquor" and "Loans" in the phone directory is "Llamas." It had once been populated by dairy and poultry farmers, but after World War II summer renters began to arrive, drawn to the dramatic coastline and the clear, bracing air. In the last ten years, more of the houses were being winterized, turned into full-time residences, so that the area is touched, here and there, with a feeling of suburbia. That's a shame. But the restaurants are much better for it. I loved the place, loved the smell of the air, the light, the sound of the surf, and the sight of what rolling farmland remained. I had never been able to spend enough time there and had long fantasized about living there. Well, here was my chance.

My house had been built in the '50s, in a quirky, modernist style, and as rooms were added in the '70s, its layout became eccentric. That was one reason the house had sat, empty, on the market for a couple of years before I was stopped in my tracks by the For Sale sign. I didn't care that you had to walk through a bathroom to get to the library. I didn't care that generations of mice had decided to call it home. I bought it. And I loved it. There was only one bedroom for the children, which they shared with their cousins, all of them curled up like small bear cubs, sleeping on futons covering the entire floor, so that by morning the room was ripe with the odor of boys.

I was as attached to that house as I had been to my New York house. When it came down to selling one or the other, I decided to keep the Rhode Island house. It was much smaller, the taxes were much lower, and it was less expensive to maintain. The children had been visiting that countryside over the course of their entire lives, but the house was really more mine. My sister, who also had a house a couple of miles away, referred to it as my hippie shack. Okay, so what if I still listen to Led Zeppelin?

I had spent copious amounts of time there by myself, after the divorce, nursing heartache, watching the birds in the meadow, swimming, reading, listening to music as I sat at my hearth, hitting repeat—repeat—repeat on my boom box as though I were still a fifteen-year-old girl. Stroller was always complimenting me on how "portable" I was—I could be plunked down into just about any situation and make my way through it with a modicum of manners. My personal inclinations tend toward hermetic. But in the course of my career I had been trained to step up to whatever plate was put in front of me. Stroller had not achieved such flexibility, evolutionarily speaking. Stroller had to have things on his terms, and he didn't much like putting himself in other people's places.

I remember the first time he made what turned out to be a five-hour drive to visit me in Rhode Island, because he insisted on leaving at the height of the rush hour. His stay lasted two hours before he made the drive home. The second time, we made a plan well in advance that he would stay for a couple of days; after all, it didn't seem fair that I could never go to my house because he could only be comfortable in his. Stroller arrived, looking a bit strained from the interstate traffic. He wouldn't come in, left his luggage in his truck, and circled the house a few times, warily. I supposed he was getting used to the contours of the place and working his way in. Eventually, he brought in a brown paper grocery bag. When I went up to the bedroom, I found that he had arranged the contents on the floor in small stacks: several books, shirts, socks, and T-shirts in neat little piles under the window.

Stroller was deeply, tenderly attached to his clothing, and

he was considerate of it. He frequently steamed his winter suits by hanging them in the bathroom with a hot shower running. He gave his blue linen summer suits (he had several, all alike) long, loving soaks in the bathtub, stirring them gently from time to time; when part of one started to unravel, he had parts of others sewn into place. He got thirty or forty years out of his suits, which you might think was a testament to excellent tailoring—and it was—but it was also a testament to the blindness of loving eyes. He liked ironing and volunteered to do my shirts. "But I don't do sheets." He liked to make a jacket feel soft and pliable, as if it had been slept in—well, it probably had been.

Stroller never traveled with enough clothing, so by the third day of any trip he was in crumpled khakis. This also meant that within days our hotel bathroom would become a laundry room, with socks wrapped around the heated towel bars and shirts dripping in the shower. He would call housekeeping for an ironing board and spend happy hours lost in a steamy reverie. He would find the complimentary sewing kit (the kind no one ever uses) tucked in a drawer and repair tears in the lining of his jackets, and then fix all the other little things that he hadn't had time to do at home. He always used the brightest color thread, pink if possible, so that his stitches, which were quite even, showed up boldly. Watching him bustle about with his clothes one evening, I realized that he had become his own nanny. It had a rather poignant charm.

The first morning of his first weekend visit to my house in Rhode Island, those many years ago, while I was straightening the bedroom, I picked Stroller's clothes up off the floor and put them on a shelf in my closet, having cleared a space in expectation of his arrival. I, too, like to have things looking a certain way, which is to say, I like clothes to be in the closet. Too many spiders lived in the baseboard. But I arranged them exactly as he did, in the same tidy stacks. Hours later, when I returned to my bedroom, Stroller's clothes had migrated back to the floor. I went downstairs to ask him what it meant.

"Were they an eyesore for you?" Stroller asked suspiciously.

"Not at all. I just didn't want you to feel like there wasn't any room for you, that I hadn't made an effort to make space."

Indeed, I had driven up ahead of time to clear off tables and shelves, still smarting from a remark he had made weeks earlier about how I occupied my house entirely—the closets were full, the rooms were furnished—proving that there was no room for anyone else. In my naïve way, I had thought that seemed healthier than leaving dismal, empty coat hangers in half the closets; filling my house was a sign that I was recovering from my divorce. I refrained from pointing out to him (for the ninety-ninth time) that his own house had not exactly welcomed me, overflowing as it was with stuff, closets bulging with discarded furniture, clothes, broken toys, cracked china, and thousands of old papers. He had had no intention of clearing anything out, and had resisted all efforts to do so for years. If I wanted room in his life, I would have to fight for it.

I had wanted to send Stroller a different message, one that welcomed him into my home, so I had cleared space ahead of his arrival. But he didn't want his clothes in my closet.

"What it means," said Stroller, "is that my clothes felt too contained in the closet. They felt closed-in. Claustrophobic. They felt trapped. I let them out."

Needless to say, the house in Rhode Island never became a part of our lives together. It was small and, mainly because it was such a structural mess, easily manageable. I never worried about it because most of the windows were already inoperable, and parts of the floor were already rotting. All it needed was a good airing out whenever I arrived.

But I had decided, three years earlier (when I was fully employed and making money), that it would be a good idea to have a functioning kitchen. I was down to one working burner; the half-size fridge squeezed into a nook carved under the stairs could barely contain the milk and eggs and orange juice the children and I needed for a weekend; and the final blow was probably when the mixer vibrated itself right off the edge of the tiny counter and, still spinning, crashed to the floor, spewing dough everywhere.

The contractor I had hired for the renovation had taken down the flimsy Sheetrock, gotten one look at the feeble two-by-fours framing the house, and refused to go any further. After pointing out more shredding wood, the sinking foundation, the mold and the insects that had taken up residence inside the walls—and my favorite item, an enormous steel beam simply floating in the wall, resting on nothing—he recommended tearing the house down and starting over. It was too dangerous. And illegal; nothing was built to code. One big hurricane, he promised, and the second floor would cave in on me. I had noticed how much the house shook in high winds, and that peculiar odor that developed when it was shut up for a few weeks had become ever more pungent.

Lesson Number One: Do not ignore rot.

I reluctantly agreed to rebuild.

It was supposed to take a year. I was in a hurry to get it done.

Lesson Number Two: Do not skimp on planning. Insist on taking the time to think things through before taking a first step; otherwise you're designing on the run.

At first, before the inevitable problems, mistakes, and delays, it was fun. I worked with the architect who had built Stroller's home and had become a friend. Dan was brilliant and affable, and had no agenda to force on me. We had to stay on the basic footprint of the old house, with only slight modification, but we could raise the height of the very low ceilings. We decided to maximize the passive solar capabilities, as the house had been thoughtfully sited decades earlier. We went with the sturdiest windows and the best insulation I could afford. The architect organized his thinking around reinterpreting the '50s style, with its boomerang shape, plate glass, and flat roof. But I didn't give him free rein—and in retrospect, there were things I would have done differently. At the time, all I wanted was my old house back, cleaned up. I wanted to be able to sit in the same spot in front of the windows, and I wanted the windows in the same places so that the views would be the same.

Lesson Number Three: Do not cling to old patterns. Nothing can ever be what it once was.

I had so enjoyed the sofa in the kitchen of my New York house that this time I put the entire living room in the kitchen; or, to put it another way, we designed one large, open room that contained a dining table, the living room furniture, and a cooking island. By the time we were done, Dan remarked that we had succeeded in building an old-fashioned New York loft in the middle of the country. We tucked a regular refrigerator, shelves, and more work space out of sight into a pantry, which looked like it belonged on a boat. The space restriction imposed discipline on me. There was room only for what was needed, one of every tool, only a few pots and pans. After all, hadn't generations of women cooked enormous meals in kitchens that were a fifth the size of what was being built these days?

Lesson Number Four: Lighten up the load you are carrying—but be prepared to battle vestigial hoarding instincts.

I could live in this one room when I was alone at the house, without the children; and when they came to visit, we would open up the rest of it. I found the whorled interior of a whelk on the beach, and in the only elaborate flourish in what was an elegant, refined modernist design, Dan used the shell as inspiration for the shape of the staircase to the second floor. It was beautiful.

Lesson Number Five: Be open to surprise. Take pleasure from the unexpected. Make room for delight.

Three years later, as I was paying the last bills to the contractor, I lost my job. But the house was ready to be inhabited.

*

I feel lucky as I begin contemplating the idea that it could be my new home. After all, if I can't find a full-time job, and I'm going to be writing, I don't have to be living in New York. But I am anxious about moving far away from Stroller, and I'm not quite ready to abandon a city I know and love. We talk about it again. I don't even want to marry him anymore, I reassure him. I just want him not to be married to someone else. It is too Oedipal, some weird variation on me stealing poor, beleaguered Daddy away from mean Mommy. I could see this was an unhealthy arrangement for me, even if Stroller couldn't. He insists that I am the one with the problem. What difference does it make that he is married?

I still have not settled this question when I call my old friend David in Charleston to get a male perspective on the situation. David hasn't been following this particular saga, but he has a refreshing way of immediately cutting through to the essence of any situation.

"You're wondering if it matters that he's married? After seven years? Are you kidding? *Single* is building standard!"

"Building standard?" I hadn't known about this particular guideline to relationships.

"Yeah. You know how when you rent office space, you get white walls, spongy acoustic tile ceilings, access to bathrooms? Running water? Heat? That's baseline. That's the *least* you can expect for your money. That is what is known as building standard. Married is *not* building standard for a guy you're dating. *Divorced* is building standard. *Single. Available.* Are you nuts? Why don't you think you're worth it, anyway?"

This is a stunning idea. I have been operating way beyond building standard for the last few years—when it has come to making a home. For that matter, I have spent my working life— at places as varied as *Esquire*, *Texas Monthly* and *Newsweek*— delivering way beyond building standard. I never doubted my basic worth to those companies; whatever insecurity I had only spurred me to do more, perform as well as I could. But when it has come to making a relationship, I have been willing to build on a shaky foundation. I suddenly realize that I am not going to think, or even argue, my way through the Stroller dilemma. I have to feel my way through and finally trust that voice inside me that insists I am not comfortable. I don't want to be without a mate forever, but it seems a good time to make some peace with what it means to have a partner.

Maybe I've been avoiding my own issues of ambivalence by being so attached to someone else's. Maybe Stroller's problems have been masking mine—maybe when we get attached to suffering, we use it to avoid our own difficult truths. Maybe it is time to stop the struggle and see what happens if I accept being alone. I start doing a trick my friend Caroline taught me. I make fists with both hands, and then unclench and relax them, holding my palms out in release. It feels fantastic, a letting go. After all, one way to complete a project is to drop it.

I am long past due for a personal renovation. But my tool-box feels empty.

WINTER DRAWS TO a close, and suddenly, as if the seasonal change in daylight has triggered a new flood of chemicals inside me, my brain flips a switch and I go from sleeping all the time to being utterly lost in sleeplessness. An impossible abyss of wakeful nights yawns open, nights of lying awake for hours, too tired to do anything at all, my mind racing. Nights of falling asleep only to wake up at the cursed hour of 4:00 A.M., too early to get out of bed, too late to drift back into precious sleep. When I talk to my friends about these sleepless nights, I learn that they are having the same problem. No one sleeps anymore. We talk about what to do. We are grouchy with sleep deprivation; we panic. What if we never sleep again? Sometimes I am so exhausted from the struggles of the night that I have little reserve for the struggles of the day.

Those sleepless nights. I try chamomile, rosemary, mint, verbena infusions. I try sitting in the empty kitchen, lights out, listening to the gentle fans of the refrigerator. I try kava. I try meditating, doodling, even reading the hammerlike prose of a high-school history textbook, so stupefying it could put me to sleep in the middle of the day. But not at night.

I have night sweats. I wake drenched, my sheets cold and clammy. I keep a pile of pajamas by the bed so I can change without getting up. Are these hot flashes? Then I'm freezing, curled in a fetal position under piles of blankets, my muscles bunched with chills. I read about premenstrual, menopausal, and peri-menopausal syndromes. I go in for blood work. My hormone levels are fine, normal, one doctor reports. I'm suspicious of his certainty. Another tells me that there are no bright lines be-tween life changes anywhere during these years, least of all in our bodies.

I try exercise during the day, a steaming bath scented with lavender at night. Nothing works. I try acupuncture, I try tarot cards, I try astrology. I throw dice and consult the *I Ching*. There are no answers. It is important to fight the sleeplessness. It is also important not to fight it. It makes no difference, either way.

I switch off the lights. I light candles. I switch on the lights. I light incense. You aren't supposed to look at the clock when you wake in the middle of the night. I don't look at the clock. But then I get fixated on figuring out the time by the position of the moon, the stars, the quality of the light. So I look at the clock. It's too early. It's too late. So what?

In exhaustion, my memory begins to falter. Black holes gape open before me as I speak; in the middle of a sentence, I grope zanily for safe passage to the next word. What was I trying to say? Sometimes I can approximate the shape of the word, or catch the first letter, but I feel as if I am kicking up piles of dead leaves; words scatter away with a dry, empty crackle.

I try making lists, as if pinning down the noisy unfurl-ing of my troubles will quiet their annoying flap. I make lists of things to do the next day. I make lists of things to do in the next year. I make lists of ways to redesign the garden. I lie under the covers and wander through new perennial beds, new stands of trees, new masses of herbs, new containers of vegetables. I pull the sheets over my head and dream up new tables, new carpets, new slipcovers. I make lists of how much all the items on these lists would cost me. I throw all the lists away.

I call a doctor who has helped me in the past, a psychoanalyst, thinking that what wakes me are deeply buried problems that are trying, awkwardly, to heave themselves up out of the rich loam of my unconscious. As soon as I make an appointment to meet with the doctor, the little bits of sleep I manage to snatch are overwhelmed by anxious dreams from which I wake, drenched again in sweat, my chest constricted, my pillow soaked with tears. All I can remember of the first bad dream is that I am trapped in my pantry, under attack, someone trying to come in through a window. With the bizarre perspective that dreams command, I see that I am the one trying to come in a window, a narrow aperture. It is a tight squeeze, and I'm watching myself come through feet first, a bright light shining in on me, like a spotlight. There you have it, finally I remember being born. But I don't get to be an infant for long. In the full glare of that light I notice a telephone hanging on the wall. I reach for it, I want to call for help, but in my panic I cannot remember what number to dial: 411? 911? 411? 911? 411? 911? Which is it? The numbers wheel through my dizzy brain, my heart races, until, mercifully, I wake.

Help? Information? What is it I need?

Help. I read aimlessly, voraciously, turning to the ancients
for help, those books of wisdom that have always given me comfort, and, at the very least, distraction: Ovid, Homer, the teach-
ings of the Buddha. I feel as if I am skating over the words with
dull blades; nothing gives me traction; nothing is as alive as it
once was. My reading is scattered, impatient, layered, nervous,
and skittering. I have nightmares about books. The words on
the page melt before my eyes, the ink slithers away, hissing.

I turn to the Bible—the black, leather-clad King James I
was given in honor of my confirmation in high school; black,
even though girls were supposed to get white, because the people filling the Bible orders assumed, as most people did, that
my name was a boy's name. But in everything I read, all that
catches my attention are those glittering shards that mirror my
unhappy state. I do not need clarification for how I feel, which
is in sharp enough relief, but there is solace in finding that I am
keeping company with others, even across the centuries.

I go all the way through the Old Testament, stunned at
the rage, vengeance, chaos, and miracles; then I work my way
through the New Testament, stunned at the faith, trust, and
miracles. I note that the Bible is a book full of fear, that over and
over again, the response to change, and even to the miraculous,
is fear. The rock is rolled back, and the discovery is met not with
joy, not elation, but fear. I begin to wonder about everything I
have missed in being fearful. It dawns on me how apt fear is, in
so many circumstances. But it isn't enough.

Yet, I feel as though I am looking at the characters through the wrong end of a telescope, which is exactly the opposite of the way I normally feel when I am reading. Here in the Bible is a world created and laid before me, a gift said to be from God's mouth to our ears, and yet at first I cannot feel much for it, besides astonishment that there are people—my aunt Kathleen included—who believe that every word in the Bible is literally true. How is it that I have strayed so far from the capacity to suspend disbelief? Here I am, ready and willing, desperate to find God, and God does not come. I admit to myself that even in my highly charged search, I do not believe that He exists. And yet, I capitalize *He*. I cannot quite bring myself to commit to lowercasing His status, relegating Him to the pantheon of the Greek or Hindu gods. It may be superstition: What if He is paying attention? What if He gets mad?

I must not be ready to find it in my heart to ask God for help, though I read the words: "Turn thee unto me, and have mercy upon me; for I am desolate and afflicted. The troubles of my heart are enlarged: O bring thou me out of my distress." Nothing seems to bring me out of my distress; there are no miraculous awakenings. Well, that's not entirely true. As I sit with that Bible in the middle of the night, I am moved by the language of the King James Bible; gorgeous, intricate, mouthy prayers blanket me in wonderment. From time to time words still have the power to touch me, and if God is the Word, perhaps in that way I am not entirely lost. But I am not comforted, either. Within weeks, it is to the Psalms that I turn most frequently in my nocturnal wanderings. The Psalms reveal a roaring world of wings and rocks, a world in which men wail and sob and tear their hair. The words roll over me, phrases crashing and returning, again and again, in endless waves.

I might not be ready to ask God for help, but the more tired I get, the more ready I am to accuse—anyone, everyone—for my troubles, and to feel abandoned and angry about it. I read and reread Psalm 22, which instantly becomes my favorite hymn of despair: "My God, my God, why hast thou forsaken me? Why art thou so far from helping me, and from the words of my roaring?" My thoughts reverberate until they reach a screaming pitch. Insomnia has kidnapped peace. These nights leave me so worn out that there are moments in the day when I feel as if I will collapse at the slightest pressure; every difficulty is amplified: "O my God, I cry in the daytime, but thou hearest me not; and in the night season, and am not silent."

I have to remind myself that I am simply tired. But there comes over me, at times, a weariness such as I have never experienced before. When I lose an entire night of sleep, I feel ill for days. There, in Psalm 22, I find an anthem for the season of sleeplessness: "I am poured out like water, and all my bones are out of joint: my heart is like wax; it is melted in the midst of my bowels."

One morning, in a panic of sleeplessness, I go downstairs to the piano, and as there's no one to wake up, I begin to pick my way through a volume of music I've had in my library for many years and never bothered to play, probably because it intimidated me. *Goldberg-Variationen*, reads the title page. The abbreviated name Joh. Seb. Bach is sprawled handsomely in large type across one line. The first piece is an aria, and a harpsichord with two keyboards—*Cembalo mit 2 Manualen*—is specified. Since I do not have one at my disposal, I sit down at the sort of instrument Johann Sebastian Bach would never have seen in his lifetime, a grand piano. I set the music up on the stand, and begin to play. The aria has a quiet, dignified, spare quality, and I find it soothing to make my way around and inside the notes. The melody is elegant, contained. The more I play through it, the more I begin to feel that the piece holds much in reserve. It seems curiously forthright and hidden at the same time. For me, it is clearly the beginning of something big—musically, of course, but emotionally, too. This isn't the first time I have heard the piece. As soon as I play the aria, I remember a couple of recordings of the *Goldberg Variations* that I bought years ago. I have not listened to them in a long time. I make a note to pull those down off the shelf so I can study the pianists' interpretations and read the liner notes. I won't be able to unlock the keys to the *Variations* by myself. Perhaps I will even find a teacher. Haven't I said for years that taking piano lessons is one of the things I want to do, if I ever find the time?

I finger my way through the pieces behind the aria, some marked *Canone, all'Unisuono, alla Seconda, alla Terza, Quodlibet*—I have no idea what all those notations mean—others marked *Giga, Fughetta*, and then an *Ouverture*, another opening right in the middle of everything. The living room is beginning to fill with the pinkish-gray light of dawn. I page ahead to find pieces marked *andante* or *adagio tempi* that I can more confidently handle. Many of the variations are dense with thirty-second notes; at that hour, the notes look frightening even on paper, bars of black lines slashing across the pages.

I am aware that my fingers do not play the way they did in high school and college, when I could spend four to six hours a day practicing. They don't move quickly, or lightly, or evenly, or powerfully. In these early hours, my fingers are stiff. What I feel is not quite pain, but beyond awareness. Within an hour, my back is beginning to ache; spasms radiate between my shoulder blades, tingle along my arms. I look down at the skin on the backs of my hands with some distress; it's looser than it once was, beginning to crackle like the glaze on old porcelain, and more transparent, so that the veins look bluer. Hands give away age. Some say that if you want to know if a woman has had plastic surgery, look at the skin on her hands compared to the skin across her cheekbones. I am the kind of person who always notices other people's hands when I first meet them; hands fascinate me. But I have never before worried about my own hands. They appear to be blooming with freckles, until I realize those are the dreaded liver spots (awful term). My nails are never polished and always trimmed to what I think of as new-moon length. These are grooming habits from my years as a music student. So I ask my poor hands: *Are you with me or against me?* Into the Bach we plunge.

Most of the pieces are in a major key, the simple G major with its one F-sharp. Of the thirty variations, only three are in a minor key; the music I have loved and returned to through decades of being a piano student is in minor keys. These Bach pieces are nothing like the Chopin nocturnes I've pored over for years, staves thick with key changes, modulations, transpositions, surprises. I have always been fatally drawn to the melancholy, the troubled. Undertow is my specialty. I was never interested in Bach—as a child, I found him tedious; as an adolescent, boring. His music was always forced on me, as part of the repertoire necessary for serious training. Playing the music of Bach—and Haydn and Mozart—felt like calisthenics. I rattled through those pieces mindlessly, having been taught, incorrectly, that there was no place for emotional expression in the classical or baroque. Bach seemed to be only about religious cheer. I imagined him to be a stern, self-satisfied trick-meister who tangled pianists' fingers in cruelly convoluted, contorted passages; his music seemed irrelevant, fussy, and cerebral—just an evolutionary stage to pass through quickly on the way to the pinnacle of the piano repertoire achieved by Brahms, Beethoven, Schumann, and Chopin. Now *that* was music that had the power to release my own adolescent yearnings, written by kindred, melancholic spirits, as I imagined them.

So I am surprised to find myself getting enormous pleasure from that little major-key aria. I can see there is much behind its beguiling simplicity. As announcements go, it strikes me as understated; it says little and contains much. As I go over and over it in those early morning hours, I begin to get it into my fingers, begin to recognize, and then anticipate, the path it cuts across the keyboard.

I don't know what drew me to that book; I must have bought the score years ago for a class I never pursued in college. Perhaps the book itself caught my eye: the dark-blue, rag-paper cover is pleasing, cleanly designed, quietly authoritative. Even the idea of an urtext edition is appealing; the heart of the matter exposed, no ornamentation added. The preface notes that the editor was able to refer to a copy of the original edition of the *Goldberg Variations* discovered in 1975, "containing corrections and editions in Bach's own hand." Surprising that such a treasure could turn up as late as that. Thrilling to imagine seeing Bach's own hand, holding the heavy sheets of a manuscript, feeling the cut of the quill in the paper, for Bach wrote only with quill pens, dipping them in ink bottles, sharpening feather after feather with his knife as he scrawled his way across the pages.

The music is doing nothing for my sleeplessness; if anything, I am more completely, wonderfully awake than I have been in a long time. Unexpectedly, I feel a peace suffuse my bones as I lose myself in Bach's lines. My own anxieties are no longer drumming through my brain; my mind, that hobbled old draft horse, has stopped loping along in the same rut it has followed night after night. It is locking into someone else's harmony, being drawn into another slipstream. And there is something profound about that harmony, I feel it immediately. It stirs deep inside of me, a hunger to know more about this music. It casts a strange enchantment over me.

I bounce through the pages for a couple of hours, sloppily, noodling through one phrase after another, carving my way through passage after passage, as if I were simply out for a walk on the beach, going wherever I feel, enjoying the sunshine and examining the patterns left in the sand by the waves and pebbles, dodging the foamy surf. I am not trying to master any of the variations, just getting a feel for them.

And finally, quiet settles over me, as if, in playing, I have taken my heart in my hands and relaxed its anxious, racing pulse. I go to my bed, lie down, and sleep.

I become fascinated by Bach's life; he seems so far away in time, but he comes alive in the music. I pore over biographies. According to stubborn legend, the *Variations* were commissioned by an insomniac count, for his harpsichordist (and Bach's student) Goldberg to play in the small hours of morning. Bach suffers the heartbreak of losing his mother when he is nine years old and is an orphan by the time he is ten. He is sent to live in an older brother's house. He is forbidden to borrow scores from his brother's library, so he furtively slips them out. The boy stays awake for nights on end, years on end, copying the sheets by candlelight, by moonlight, until he has absorbed the architecture of music. Bach lives in a Europe that is consumed with an almost mystical love of numbers, a belief that mathematics will reveal the harmony underlying the disorder of the human world. He is an extraordinarily skilled keyboard player, a show-off, a jokester, a punster. His contemporaries complain about the terrific difficulty of his compositions. He fights with his patrons; he has a temper. He is lusty. He walks. And walks. He seems to think nothing of walking hundreds of miles to hear a recital. During one of his long journeys, his wife dies; she is the mother of their seven children, only four of whom survive. Bach does not even know she has been ill until he returns home, only to find her long buried. How can he not have been stricken with grief? He marries again in a year; his wife becomes pregnant twelve times and loses eight infants. Do we really believe, as we are taught, that people did not feel the loss of children so deeply then, just because it happened more frequently? And could it really be true, as again we are taught, that no trace of his life is in his music? I feel pain, heartache, yearning, love, joy, song, and pleasure all over the pages of the *Variations*. How to express any of this is left up to the player.

I begin to look for recitals of the *Goldberg Variations*. One performance I attend is strangely unsatisfactory; the audience is grumpy as we make our way up the aisles.

"He didn't even take the repeats," someone near me says. "How is that possible, not to take the repeats? Anyone who doesn't take the repeats doesn't really love Bach."

I blush. Ever since I was a child, I have always ignored those musical notations to go back and start over. Play it again? But I just did that part! From that moment on, I religiously, worshipfully, prayerfully take the repeats, because I really do love Bach. I become superstitious about it, always doubling back through each variation.

Taking the repeats turns out to have a big impact on the rest of my life. I find myself taking the repeats when I put on a recording, as I don't hear half of what has been played the first time around. Then I find myself taking the repeats in conversation, so that I am listening more carefully. I want to take the repeats in relationships with people; I am becoming more patient, less judgmental. I am paying more attention, focusing more. I take the repeats wherever I walk—in the garden, along the shore, in the woods. My life, if I am to live it properly, is suddenly full of necessary repeats.

And cadences. I begin to think of the chords Stroller and I struck, and the strange progressions we created: perfect, false, full, imperfect, transient, deceptive, interrupted, irregular, terminal. How many times did we rehearse those patterns? And how could I reach the final form, the plagal, the amen cadence? Let it be.

One night, while I'm at the keyboard, I recall a student of my own in a music class I taught in the local public high school in the early '70s. I once thought I would become a piano teacher. I was seventeen, lazy as a pianist, aware that I would have trouble teaching because I was impatient with other people's laziness. I was dimly aware, too, that I was beginning to lose touch with any pleasure I had ever taken from making music. That summer the town was sponsoring a music class, as a form of therapy, for "troubled" children. One of my students, a nine-year-old boy, was afflicted with a brain tumor. He had had several operations, and by the time he was in my class his head was swathed in bandages. What hair he had left was dark, and his eyes in his gaunt, quiet face were large and dark. He had remarkably long eyelashes, I remember. Every day, he sat at the same desk in the front row.

One shortcoming of this public education program was that there were no pianos in the classrooms, nor any other instruments for that matter, so it was hard to figure out how, exactly, to convey the musicality of making music. I managed to bring in a xylophone, a guitar, a drum, and a tambourine; of course we could also sing, and my pupils could beat time on their desks. My bandage-swathed student always kept very still, doodling with a fat pencil or gazing at me while lost in thought. He grew paler as the summer progressed. One day, at the end of class, he presented me with a drawing on a white sheet of blue-lined paper torn from his notebook. He told me he wanted me to have a picture of us. We were under the bubble of a flying-saucer type of vessel; I was at the steering wheel and he was seated behind me. I looked serious, intent on driving. He was smiling. My long, dark hair was held away from my face by the beaded headband I wore across my forehead, which, as I think about it, must have looked like a small, colorful version of the artist's own bandage. My hair was streaming around him and out of the space capsule, escaping from the dome that arched over us, like a net trawling the skies, catching stars. And, the child said, pointing to me in the drawing—I clearly remember the triumph and adoration in his voice—I was wearing a mink coat that he had given me. We were flying away together.

The child did not return the next day, and I never saw him again. He had been my best student. I don't remember that he ever struck a note or found a beat, but he had understood the gravity and joy and release of making music.

*

Over time, I grow accustomed to a new kind of slumber. I go to the piano nightly and begin to teach myself all over again how to practice. I am becoming, once again, an amateur musician. I am playing for my own pleasure, and I am learning to silence the critic in my head, the one who will not stop telling me that nothing I do is good enough, that I have not practiced enough. I try not to care if I miss notes. I know I cannot reach the tempo. What my fingers lack in speed, my heart makes up in feeling. If I have to, I will crawl through the sarabandes and the quadrilles, letting the dance fill my soul.

I am free to play at all hours; there is no one to disturb. When I wake again at the ungodly hour of 4:00 A.M., I go to the kitchen to prepare a bowl of steaming, milky, buttered Cream of Wheat. This was my favorite dinner when I was a child. Now, again, I need the reassurance that I know how to take care of myself, feed my physical hunger. I am making my peace with the night season. I have transformed these quiet hours of feeling alone in a dark world into a time of exploration, with uninterrupted concentration, the stirrings of spiritual need. I am, by now, obsessed with the *Goldberg Variations*. I listened to Bach's music for fifty years before I finally heard it.

I open the blue music book and read through the notes, singing them quietly to myself even as I play. They are deeply, reassuringly familiar, and still they retain the eloquence I responded to the first time. Here, then, is my mother's biggest gift to me: music. She was my first teacher. I think back on a concert we once attended together, a performance of a Rachmaninoff piano concerto. She took my hand and squeezed it, and when the concert was over, she turned to me and said, "All my life I wanted to be with someone who would feel the music the way I did."

She did not get this in a husband; perhaps she has it in a daughter. I am finding, in these night hours, that I am highly receptive, porous, stripped of any of the qualities that protect me from what would surely be the madness of living fully, constantly moved by real beauty, real pain. Lines of poetry that I have loved over the years float into my consciousness. "*Go. Go. Go said the bird. Human kind cannot bear very much reality.*" Words and notes— there seems to be no difference in my hearing them played, or reading them off the page, I am so fluent at this hour—have the capacity to penetrate so deeply that my entire being, brain and heart and body, are converging in a powerful harmony.

Now when I return to the Bible, I feel the strength and durability of the poets, drawn from the terrible need in their prayers.

"The Lord is nigh unto them that are of a broken heart."

"They that sow in tears shall reap in joy."

What I have found, in these hours of sleeplessness, is something I may have once encountered as a teenager, and then lost in the frantic skim through adulthood—the desire to nourish my soul. I do not have the temerity to think I have found God; I think instead that I have stumbled into a conversation that I pray will last the rest of my life. I suppose that is up to me.

It is true that nothing works the way it used to. I cannot move my hands through the music the way I hear it in my head. But every once in a while, I accomplish a passage gracefully. Fingers dance over keys, producing a sound that is light and clear. I take all the repeats. I observe the rests. I enjoy myself. I am happy for small-boned miracles.

Spring

Create in me a clean heart.

—PSALM 51:10

11. PACKING THE BOOKS

SPRING BLOWS IN so wildly that it seems unnatural, or perhaps I just notice what spring really feels like once I'm not sealed in an office building all day. Weather—the actual experience of it, not the forecast—is one of the more dramatic discoveries that comes with slowing down the pace of my life. (Weather, like cooking, is something we can now watch on a screen rather than actually experience.) There were days, in my climate-controlled office life, when I didn't even know whether it had been muggy or cool, or if it had rained. I didn't realize how out of touch with the weather I had become until I began waking with the sun, watching the fog bead the screens, feeling the floorboards and cabinet doors warp in the damp heat. It dawns on me that there is something unsavory about having been so cut off from the natural world that I am surprised by the golden hue in the slant of light at four in the afternoon, on a weekday, no less.

I started thinking about light after seeing a show of paintings by Pierre Bonnard at the Metropolitan Museum of Art. My friend Frances made one of her most helpful gestures by insisting that we go to museums and look at art. She was right: museums are restful, healing, grounding, inspiring places of refuge. The hot, dry sunshine of southern France that Bonnard was able to capture in his still lifes sustained me for weeks through the last days of winter; I returned to look at the paintings again and again, something I had not done in thirty years, and took friends with me. I had to teach myself all over again how to look at art, to slow down, contemplate, focus, and drift, not do the fast walk-through, checking the show off the media's collective must-see list.

After months of depressed sloth, I begin to walk for miles every day. I find that I think more fluidly when I'm moving, and that there is something pleasurable about being a body in motion again. Much of the time I'm not thinking about anything in particular. I begin suggesting to my working friends, still sealed in their buildings, that we take walks at lunchtime, so that I can show them the carpets of snowdrops in Central Park, or the swelling buds of the cherry trees.

And at home, I take to wandering around in my garden at all hours. As if to give me one last chance to change my mind about selling the house, the garden is unfolding more splendidly than I have ever seen. The daffodils have multiplied generously and spilled across the front in a riot of gold and orange. The hellebores, mature now, and so happy to have well-drained feet at the top of the drive, appeared in March and have kept nodding their prim white, mauve, and purple caps for more than two months; when I bend down to turn up a small head and peer into a quiet, trusting face, I wince at the thought of leaving them vulnerable to whatever depredations a new (non-)gardener will undoubtedly visit upon them. I apologize in anticipation.

I walk slowly along the paths, examining the thick, furry spools of the unwinding ferns; the stubby purple fingers of the peonies pointing up from the damp, fragrant earth; the green stumps of the Solomon's seal; the sharp tips of the hostas encircled by improbably large patches of bare ground that will soon enough be hidden in the shade of their gigantic leaves, bearing aloft the fragrant white wands that seduce the moths at dusk.

Then, one morning, I wake in a ruthless mood: why are my things in control of me, rather than the other way around? It is time to face up to the job of packing. Worse: time to cull the books.

I'm a reader, that's all there is to it. I spent a fraught childhood with my nose in a book. I could become so lost in a story that I would absentmindedly eat anything near me; once I sucked down an entire tube of toothpaste. I know that I am seriously depressed when I can no longer concentrate enough to read, unable to leave my own head long enough to get into someone else's world. I pick up Wodehouse when I want a good laugh, Edith Wharton or Henry James when I want to cry, Melville for a religious experience, and Trollope when I want to convince myself that it is possible to live in a world governed by right and wrong choices, where those who act properly get a happy ending and those who act badly suffer. When I read, everything makes sense. Sometimes the world in a book seems more real than the world in which I live.

Everyone who visits my house asks me, "Have you read all those books? Are you planning to read them?" The answer,

I hope, is no. I have been hoarding books against old age. I'm constantly thinking that one day, when I'm unable to move, paralyzed by a stroke, I'll want to plow through that enormous biography of George Eliot. Finally, I must face the fact that I am never going to read it. I'd rather read *Middlemarch* again, given the time. And that's what it's all about: time. How much time will I be given? Of course, I'll never know, and having dodged death's bullet once, I'm well aware of how arbitrarily it comes. Still, this entire exercise of getting rid of books is predicated on understanding, and accepting, that there is very little time left to read everything I want to read, even if I have (at the outside) thirty or forty more years. This is upsetting, until I confront the bookcases, when it becomes liberating.

No, I am not going to read Foucault on sexuality, not ever. Even today I cannot bear to read two pages of it, the writing is so turgid and jargon-laden. When did I think he was heroic? How glad I am to let that go. But sell that fat, heavy, volume of Heidegger's *Being and Time*? Not on your life. I was once so enamored of Heidegger that I had dreams about him, dreams of huge, long, gorgeous scrolls covered with calligraphy—the book lover's tattoos—bearing down on me as I slept . . . I've tried several times to reread *Being and Time*, and was startled to discover the overenthusiastic yellow highlighting I did as a college student. How can every sentence on a page be significant? Compared to what? Today the sentences are incomprehensible to me. I might as well be reading the original German edition. To have read that book, it was necessary to be an impressionable nineteen-year-old philosophy student, ardently following a wise and worldly professor—herself all of twenty-nine years old. Still, I'll keep it as a beloved souvenir of the person I might have became.

The worst disappointments are the cookbooks. I have six shelves of them, and of those, I have only ever regularly used three—books, that is. The rest stand in testament to the idea other people have of me as someone who ought to be able to throw a dinner party for twenty, serving braised goose with port and vegetables. I have books of recipes for Moroccan, Indian, Ethiopian, Chinese, and Japanese cuisine, and of course French and Italian. I long ago decided that this sort of book is not meant for cooking. It is, instead, food pornography. Gorgeous photographs of impossibly perfect dishes set out on impossibly perfect tables—none of which a mere mortal could ever duplicate, because it took at least five mortals, and lots of light meters, and Photoshop, to make those pictures look as enticing as they do. I should know. I spent thirteen years working with the people who do this sort of thing. Mind you, lots of talent, creativity, and craft go into the production of food pictures for books and magazines. They create stories meant to instruct and inspire, if not a turn at the stove, at least a shopping trip for new china. They are meant to make you feel like you are seated in proximity to an experience of wonderful food. No one's personal table actually makes you want to pack your bags and move to Hong Kong to learn to cook.

But the fantasies triggered by cookbooks are unending and exhausting. I definitely feel like I have cooked a twelve-course dinner by the time I have thumbed through Marcella Hazan's book, and, given her tone, I feel she is snickering at the disgraceful ignorance I'm displaying by merely glancing at the pages. However, hers is one book I will keep, as her roasted chicken is the only chicken dish I have successfully reproduced. A stern teacher can be a good thing. Reading a cookbook is akin to starting a graduate course in linguistics in the middle of the semester. All the terms already had been defined in those classes you missed. In fact, everyone seems to be fluent in some form of English other than the English you know and love. All the techniques were explicated long ago, so you are out of your depths. Blanch the fava beans? Say what?

Cooks are a bossy lot. I suppose they have to be, playing with fire and throwing knives around and all that. They are like sailors. You have to do exactly what they say in the instant of hearing it, or you're overboard. This may be an effective management style on the water or near the flames, but it is hardly helpful when you are in your own home, curled up on a sofa, surrounded by cookbooks, looking for a simple recipe. I've noticed a direct correlation between the gorgeousness of a photo shoot and the sternness of tone, as if the cook knows you are going to fail at the *gefuellte tauben* (that's stuffed pigeons to you and me) and is preparing a case of "I told you so." The only book exempt from this principle is Julia Child's *The Way to Cook*. Who else tells you how to pronounce *quiche* (keesh) and how to skip the pesky crust preparation when making one? I believe she loved eggs as much as I do. From that book I learned to make a soufflé, and whenever I pull it down off the shelf, it falls open to the pictures of "Attaching the Collar" and "Removing the Collar," though I never included collars in my dinner productions and it never mattered. Holding that book brings back memories of racing home from work to make cheese soufflés for the boys: for years they were delighted by the puffy creations, by the whisper of air escaping when I pulled apart the top to serve dinner. I was always amazed that it worked. In fact, I interrupt my packing to whip up another soufflé to see if I still have it in me. I do. I needed that breath of air.

Back to sorting and packing. My throat catches at the sight of *The Silver Palate Cookbook*. I remember the store that inspired the book opening in 1977 (the same year I moved to New York after college), around the corner from my first apartment. I used my stove for heat in the winter, and took home from the Silver Palate small, precious portions of dinner. Their book came out in the early '80s; my copy became stained and well-thumbed— by my husband. I used it as escapist literature. It captured the essence of the yuppie obsession with creating sophisticated American food, giving recipes kicky and celebratory titles like Herbed Bluefish Flamed with Gin, or Wall Street Soufflé.

Back then, food processors were still something of a novelty item in the average kitchen. The book is full of recipes for desserts blended with amaretto, bourbon, and Armagnac, including what now look like quaint pieces introducing the reader to Burgundy and to Bordeaux, "the most important wine region in France." Remember when that was a discovery? These days there isn't a college student who doesn't know about Bordeaux, because the Food Network is running nonstop on dormitory televisions. And there isn't a deli that doesn't serve chicken salad with grapes and pecans, but when the Silver Palate introduced it at their shop, it was a surprise. So were oatmeal chocolate-chip cookies. And Chicken Marbella, a dinner party staple, could make anyone feel like a sophisticated host.

The Silver Palate Cookbook seems so hopelessly dated now, so '80s, but it ushered in an age of cooking competitiveness that still hasn't ended; in fact, it got more men, bringing their scoreboards with them, back into the kitchen. Has anything really changed now that we're hankering for simple food? We're just becoming competitively simple. I notice that the same people who espouse principles of respect for natural ingredients and easy preparations turn up their noses in disdain when meals aren't prepared, or even presented, their way. At least the Silver Palate ladies had a hearty sense of enthusiastic pleasure. Forget Simone de Beauvoir and Betty Friedan. I left them behind as soon as I left school. *The Silver Palate Cookbook* is the only book that perfectly captured my hopes, as a young, single, working woman in New York, for the kind of accomplished person I would grow up to be. But I haven't turned to it in thirty years.

Why would I move into my next life with 160-odd cookbooks that make me feel as if I'll never measure up in the kitchen? They make me feel worse than Heidegger does. I put them all in a giveaway pile, holding back only Marcella Hazan, because it makes me smile to remember how my husband used to say, "I'll do whatever Marcella says . . ." I keep a couple of bread books as souvenirs of the '70s, when you couldn't eat decent bread unless you made it or lived in Paris.

I pack up at least thirty boxes of books and seal them with heavy tape. The owner of the small local bookstore, the kind of place one wants to support, has agreed to come get them. Naturally, he doesn't show up. While the boxes sit in the hall for a few weeks, I begin to worry that I was ruthless in my culling, that I might have thrown away too much of my history, too much of my hope for the future of my mental life. What if I'm paralyzed for thirty years? That would leave a lot of time for reading. My books start feeling like phantom limbs. I suddenly need to refer to one—I know exactly where it is on the shelf, but when I reach for it, it's gone.

The cardboard boxes of my reading life sit impassively in the front hall, glowering at me; I'm riddled with guilt. My resistance and fortitude collapse, and late one night, in a panic of loss, I slit open the brittle packing tape and paw through the boxes. What could I have been thinking? Giving away Gisele Freund's charming *Three Days with Joyce*? Such a slim volume surely can be squeezed in somewhere. Or that tiny paperback copy of May Sarton's *Journal of a Solitude*, so yellow with age that the pages don't even tear, they crack. A gift card slips out, from my ex-mother-in-law, but no date. Did it arrive after the divorce? How cutting of her. Did it arrive before? How could she have known? Of course I'm keeping all the magic of Alice Hoffman, even though my sister wants those books. And was I out of my mind to part with *The Silver Palate*? Surely there is time left; I can give myself one last chance to try my hand at Banana Bourbon Cake with Bourbon Crème Anglaise.

Goodbye, though, once more to the biographies of Hegel and Wittgenstein. Goodbye to A. J. Ayer's *Philosophy in the Twentieth Century*. And this time, for good, farewell to Donald Keene's *Travelers of a Hundred Ages: The Japanese as Revealed Through 1,000 Years of Diaries*. I think less of myself to realize I am a person who will never make time to read these books. But I also feel relieved to have taken one last detour through my boxes. I decide to keep *The Walker's Guide to Snowdonia*. Even if I never get there, I can unfold the map and gaze with wonder at the expansive green landscape, perfect for the solitaries among us, tracing the routes with my finger—wishing, indeed, that I had a walking map for the next few decades.

12. MOVING ON

ONE GORGEOUS LATE-SPRING morning, the garden offering up masses of peonies as if in a curtain call, a moving van pulls into the driveway.

"Lady, this is way more than a small truck of stuff." The moving guy walks through the dining room and the living room, both of which look spare to my eye. "Did you *add* stuff since we gave you that bid?"

No, I have been giving things away, sending sofas, armchairs, carpets, curtains, and china to friends and family. Yet there still seems to be a lot, I have to admit. The movers manage to squeeze it all into their truck (okay, I confess, they have to add another small one) and drive off to Rhode Island.

After the vans leave, I take a last lingering walk through the empty rooms of my no-longer Forever House, stroke one last wall, give it another final kiss, and say goodbye to my life, which now seems to be unspooling in reverse. This marks the end of days with small children, the end of digging in my garden—the end of an attachment to a home I have loved so passionately. The door is, literally, closing. So are the windows. Everything is shutting down. What strikes me most are all the dry, dusty, fur-balled patches on the floors, left behind by the beds and bureaus, where the vacuum cleaner never reached in all those years—as good a sign as any that the time had come to move the furniture. I back down the drive, one last time, over that tricky bump, and head north.

It seems only fitting that, as I pull away from the old house, the skies occlude and torrential rains greet us in Rhode Island.

When we get to the new house, I am paralyzed with indecision about what goes where. Has the house gotten smaller since I last saw it? The movers have no patience.

"Lady, just tell us where to put the boxes. This place is a friggin' swamp. You can change everything after we leave." They stack the boxes as high as they can reach. No one stops to think about how I am going to get them down.

For days, the coastal skies are dull and heavy. The arrival in Rhode Island of a veritable avalanche of stuff from the old house upends the sanctity of the new, empty vessel into which I am moving. I liked the spare, spacious look of my new house, a clean slate, and I didn't even mind sleeping on a mattress on the floor while I was waiting for my old bed to arrive. But now my sunny rooms have become a poorly organized warehouse.

I let everything marinate, not ready to face the job of unpacking. But over the last thirteen years, I have done enough thinking about how to make houses into homes, and how to live well by turning a home into a sanctuary, that I know not to spend too much time among the cardboard boxes. Besides, they are beginning to smell. (There is something about the way cardboard is constructed: once damp, it not only never dries, but also retains an indelible moldy odor. I'm sure there is some really good industrial application for material with these qualities.)

With the move, I have sprung loose all the stuff that I hastily packed from my *House & Garden* office and piled in the closets of my old home. Dozens of cardboard boxes contain thirteen years worth of files, books, papers, letters, miscellaneous office supplies, pantyhose, sweaters, reading glasses—plus armchairs, tables, a desk, carpets. It smells like a few things have broken. An odor wafts from one box, suspiciously reminiscent of Femme Rochas, a rancid version of its former self. I inherited a love of perfume from my mother, who, being French, did not consider herself completely dressed until she had applied perfume, lots of it, and tied a silk scarf around her neck. A colleague once told me that she was sure my head would fall off if I ever stopped wearing a scarf, so I stopped wearing one. And see what happened? I lost my head.

A mysterious blue-black stain is slowly spreading across the bottom corner of another box at the top of the pile. I get up on a chair and slowly ease the box down to the floor to open it. A plastic bottle of Windex had cracked under the pressure of all the paper piled on it. Windex—and you know what that smells like—has leaked into the files, which have absorbed it like blotting paper. There is no type left on any of the papers in those files. The ink has dissolved and washed away into the cardboard. It is so brutally symbolic: the files were stuffed with police reports and records of bank disputes involving a case of identity theft. My identity.

I toss the sodden wad into the trash, and then sit on the floor to contemplate the enormity of all this unpacking. That's when I take a hard look around at my new house. I am trying to follow the advice I used to give my readers: *do not wallow*. Especially in times of crisis, it is imperative that you hang curtains, polish the floor, and furnish, furnish, furnish, so that you aren't coming home to empty, dismal rooms that make you feel that you have no life. Turn on the lights at once. Pull together a bouquet of flowers, even if you have to stop at traffic medians to pick them. Rooms that feel like no one is living in them send the wrong signal to your brain. I also decide to take my mother's advice—*make an effort*.

In spite of all my work with the moving men, arranging furniture from my old house, my new house has not become a home. Part of the problem, I think, as I look around at the boxes everywhere, is that I have not put out all the souvenirs of my old life: the photographs of the children, the little clay art pieces—snakes and birds and foxes—that the boys brought home from kindergarten, all my books, and (I hate to say it) the knickknacks that I cherish. The New York realtor's words are still ringing in my ears. She was right. Empty surfaces enable you to imagine a life in the rooms. Here I am, imagining, but my life has remained boxed up. Time to move in.

I confess to having been intimidated. The biggest problem with spending years with professionals of supposedly impeccable taste is that you eventually experience an erosion of your own sensibilities. Decorators have frequently told me, rolling their eyes, about clients who have so little confidence that they ask to be given diagrams for each tabletop—literally indicating where to place the lamp, the Venetian paperweight, the pile of

books, the candle—sort of like a landscape plan for interior surfaces. I have always thought designers dislike clients who are so
dependent, so needy, that they become an unnecessary burden.
I've heard about clients who can't even buy their own toothpaste
and shaving cream because they have become paralyzed by the
unremitting standards set by their decorators. This is particularly true of single, male clients who, until they hire a decorator,
have depended on wives or girlfriends to select and set out the
bath salts and shampoo bottles.

My favorite revelation along these lines came during a visit
to an exquisite and palatial Park Avenue apartment; I got to the
perfect replica of an Edwardian bathroom, with nickel fixtures
and marble counters, and there, by the sink, next to the exactly correct dish of perfect, smooth, eggshell-colored soaps, the
boar bristle shaving brush in its polished stand, and the discreet
silver tube of toothpaste that probably cost twelve dollars—
alongside this carefully crafted, intimate landscape of exquisite
taste was a crumpled, oozing tube of Crest, a cheap, disposable
plastic razor, and a can of Barbasol, complete with rusted rim.
The decorator averted his gaze, quickly ushered me out of the
room, and made a remark to the effect of "incorrigible, wealthy
boors." So much for respecting personal preferences.

As I was saying, I have always assumed that the professionals resent this level of dependence, this decorating-induced
coma, in their clients. But now, looking around my house, I realize that the reverse is true. They have us exactly where they want
us: crippled by insecurity, dependent on guidance from on high,

embarrassed by the debris of the lives we lived before we were saved, and generally unable to make a move without picking up the phone for reassurance and step-by-step guidance. I, too, who spent years telling readers to be confident—*Do your own thing! Listen to your inner designer! Don't be afraid! Express yourself!*—have fallen prey to the mystique of professional design. I am living proof of what we all fear: being held in judgment for sub-par taste. I have become fearful of buying a thing without getting approval from someone else, someone I'm not even married to, someone who isn't even living with me! What power!

Before I got into the home-decorating racket, I was more capable of making a home for myself, of knowing, instinctively, what made a house feel like a home. And that had nothing to do with professionalism; it had to do with a simple, effortless accumulation, over many years, of habits of living. My basic decorating rule of thumb is to create as many lovely places in which to sit and read as possible. By this time in my life, I need a certain kind of chair and a certain kind of table nearby, a place on which to prop my feet, and a kind of light that suits my eyes. I like a certain color palette. I need a kind of comfortable clutter; I like to rest my eyes on things, to remember the times I found them or the people who gave them to me. And when I'm tired of them, I box them up for storage, so that when I unpack them years later, they can surprise me once again.

I have never met a designer who was willing to fold into their egg-white omelets the yolks of a past life. No matter what it is, somehow it doesn't suit. This isn't completely unreasonable.

Much of what I had in my old house doesn't suit the proportions of the new rooms. But I am attached to certain pieces, small tables and chairs. After seeing the stricken look on my architect's face the first time he confronts one of my chairs, I become abject. No, I certainly did not mean to keep that chair, an antique that my in-laws gave me as a wedding gift. It was simply holding a place for a new antique, one he would help me find. Did I neglect to mention that? So sorry.

It isn't even clear why I need furniture at all. It only seems to mangle the sight lines of the rooms. Then I understand. Great designers have a vision that is all-encompassing. This is why you are mistaken if you think you are calling in a designer for a bit of help with color or a few pieces of furniture. It never stops there; it cannot. A good designer has an airtight visual lock on the world he or she wants to see, and that's that. A designer may sincerely want to make room for a few of a client's old pieces, but it never seems to work that way; when push comes to shove, out they go.

And so I shed the professional insecurity and begin the project of setting up a new home, rehabilitating my things. I dial a good rock station on the radio, and while Annie Lennox walks on broken glass, I tackle the office boxes. I am opening boxes late into the night. I set up files in the kitchen and spread the contents of bins and drawers onto the floor to see where I can put them, if I'm keeping them. I am astonished at how much stuff I accumulated at work over the decades. I don't even recognize half of it. Honestly, I am astonished to realize that, after the boys left home, I began living at the office. I unpack with more and more excitement. There are the photographs of the children that I propped up on the ledge behind my desk; there are the polished rocks that I played with while on the phone; there is the old green-glazed ginger jar in which I kept my pencils. I even find a small box full of Theo's old Lambie, the love object of his babyhood that began as a sheepskin rug but was slowly, under the pressure of his tiny but cherishing fingers, rubbed so fine that it shredded into dozens of pieces. How could I throw those away, even though he had? I had needed their comforting presence at work.

I begin placing things on tables around the house. I put my old garden books on the empty shelves. I put Lambie's remains in my sock drawer. I find room for all the perfume and lipstick and clothing I used to keep in closets at the office because it was easier to change there for evening events than to come all the way home and go back out again. The truth was, if I ever got home, I wouldn't leave again.

As I spend the next few days arranging my beloved things throughout my rooms, a feeling of calm contentment settles over me. I mix up some vinegar and water to clean a glass table; I wipe down some dusty books and rinse out my office teacups. When I get tired of housework, I go out into the garden to work. There I have digging and pruning and planting to last a lifetime.

Miraculously, as soon as my books are organized and my desk is polished, as soon as my shovel hits the dirt, I begin to write again. Without missing keys. It is a pleasure to be reunited with words. When my literary agent phones to see how I am doing with the move, I lament the state of the magazine business and tell her how afraid I am that I will never work again. Then I tell her what I am writing.

"You're writing?" she says. "See? You're working."

And so I am, though I haven't thought of it that way, with no one telling me what to do, no one but me to organize my time. I am astonished at how happy I am at the keyboard. Once I get going, all those years of magazine deadlines give me plenty of discipline. All those years of editing give me confidence: just get the words down, they can always be changed.

I am deciding not only where home is going to be, but also how I am going to live there. I hate to be the one to bring up silver linings, or worse, windows opening while doors are slamming shut, but even I have to admit that something good is happening. All the activity is distracting, and more: it is soothing and settling. No, it is better than that: it is life-defining. Odd that being fired from a job about making homes would finally make it possible for me to make a new home in a place I have long wanted to know better. I feel a small flash of liberation. I am no longer afraid to make a very big move.

13. HERBAL REMEDIES

THE LAND AROUND my house in Rhode Island looks exactly like what it is, a construction site. Whenever the wind comes up, dirt devils whirl across the back, and unless I keep the windows shut, I'll spend hours with the vacuum cleaner. By late spring we are in a searing drought, so there is no point in planting grass until the rains come again. Instead, I plant ten or twelve pots of mint in a grid around the backyard, which is exposed to full sun every day, year-round.

When I ask a lawn guy to give me an estimate for planting grass seed, he looks over the yard and says, "What, I'm supposed to plant the grass around the mint?" I assure him that isn't my expectation, that I want the mint simply to trail through the grass. However, it's taking such a long time for the lawn guy to do his job—and the rain guy to do his—that the straggly stalks of mint are turning into sizeable mounds, sending runners in every direction through the bare soil. It has even begun to form a ragged border around the terrace by the kitchen door. At least it is holding down what passes for topsoil.

The mint thing starts because I want mint for my tea, and the local farm stand has run out of it. I go to the nursery to buy some plants, figuring I can just grow my own. But it takes me a while to get around to putting them in the ground; I just clip off the tops and keep the pots watered. There is nothing mint doesn't enhance. It even gives my favorite old standby, Cream of Wheat, a little kick every now and then. On top of having a powerful fragrance, mint, like rosemary and ginger, does wonders for one's digestion. I am fast becoming a scholar in the art of tisanes, infusions of herbs that are said to have medicinal value. A stalk of lemon verbena in a pitcher of cold water provides refreshment and healthful benefits all day; so does an infusion of rosemary in boiling water. Slices of cucumber in a glass of cold water is a remedy for bloating. Herbs, by the way, crushed and mixed with sea salt and almond oil, are just as delicious for your skin in a hot bath as they are for your palate.

I leave the house for a week to visit friends, and by the time I return the mint is burnt to a frazzle. I go to the nursery and buy a couple more pots, and this time put them in the ground immediately, throwing the charred stalks of the first pots into the holes for fertilizer. The new plants are so desperate to spread forth that they are bursting from their plastic containers; the runners have already gone several laps around the rim of the pots and then twined themselves into the neighboring pots so that I have to rip them apart to plant them. One afternoon, coming back from a walk, I accidentally step on the mint, and it releases a sharp, heady bouquet. That pleases me enormously, so I plant a few more pots, thinking that a lawn of mint might be an excellently fragrant and original landscaping concept. To my astonishment, even the fried remains of the original pots begin to show signs of life, becoming as prolific as their mates within weeks.

They are vigorous, to say the least.

Some might say invasive.

Even the grass, finally sown, is having a hard time competing with the mint. Every once in a while, looking out over my mint plantation, I wonder what has possessed me. Sure, the infusion thing. But that isn't the real story. The truth is that I planted the mint everywhere because there was no longer anyone around to tell me that I couldn't.

Mint had a lot to do with my relationship with Stroller. Back in the days when he and I tried to work out a way to live together, we were spending most weekends at his house in the country. After fits and starts, after many lunar cycles had wheeled through the skies, he finally took the giant step of promising to finalize his divorce. He had done the hardest part with the legal separation. But nothing happened; he remained reluctant to resolve matters. After years, he still couldn't see why I would care that he was married. I still couldn't see why, if the marriage was meaningless, he would want to stay married. It was a confusing mess, until its perverse logic dawned on me. By staying married to a woman he was no longer attached to, and being attached to a woman he could never marry, he was able to maintain a harmony of perfect ambivalence. It worked for him.

Thinking back on it as I gaze over my minty lawn, I see that every time he decided to let go of his ambivalence, he began throwing up new barricades against me. It is obvious to me, now, that our problems weren't coming from his inability to make a clean break from his marriage; they were symbolic of a larger inability to relax into a peaceful, loving relationship, one that didn't include shoving me away with stunning regularity. The mere proximity to a vital, unambiguous attachment triggered calamity in his heart. I wish I could say this was unusual, but I know too many women navigating the same perilous waters. Stroller's wife, for one. And I know too many men whose response to all of this would be, Hey, what's the problem here?

I spent years trying to figure out how to live with Stroller; you can see that it might have been tricky. His ambivalence spilled into our relationship in countless ways. He wanted me to live with him, in his house, but he wouldn't let go of anything from his past life without a fight. What is it about people who don't understand that furniture is stuffed with meaning? Not springs. Not feathers. Not foam. What's inside every chair, sofa, and mattress is history. Significance. We've all had the experience of getting a funny feeling when walking into a room, only to find out later that it was the scene of a terrible crime, or that it belonged to a couple in the middle of a divorce. Furniture has karma. Some stuff just feels haunted; there is another, unseen, perhaps not-so-benign presence under certain beds. There is, in fact, an entire specialty among psychics having to do with reading signs in objects. I don't know why people bother to wonder what stories the walls would tell if they could speak. As far as I'm concerned, the furniture's already yelling.

Not letting go of the bed you shared with your spouse is a pure and uncomplicated sign, as divination goes. It says that you are not moving on. People leave, but they cannot move. And the furniture says it all.

I can't tell you how many couples I know who have decorating problems that have nothing to do with taste and everything to do with stuck hearts and minds. By middle age, all new relationships begin with a lot of baggage—and we thought we had lots of it when we were teenagers. It is a shock to understand now that all that was mere carry-on, knapsacks, compared to what we are hauling around by the time we are in our fifties. And there is no such thing as curbside checking, or scanners that tell you whether anything volatile is in that baggage.

Does that mean you should start every new relationship with a yard sale—get rid of everything, wipe out that karma? We all know that's impossible. You'd still have a callus on your heart from carrying it all around for so long. There is no such thing (nor should there be) as a clean slate. There is only clean enough to move on; clean enough for a fresh inscription; clean enough to give someone else a turn to leave a mark. This means you need a sense of discernment about what goes and what stays. And you know what? Moving the marriage bed to another room doesn't cut it.

One of the hardest things about being part of a couple is that you have to agree on so many things: what color to paint the walls, where to hang the art, what art, what table, what lamp, what carpet. I mean, it is endless. You can't just go out and buy yourself a chandelier. Someone else has to approve of it. You can't just go out and buy yourself a house. Someone else has to like it as much as you do. Even, perhaps especially, if you are paying for it. Otherwise, you are controlling. Of course, everyone wants to be in control. Does "she is out of control" sound like a compliment?

Sharing and agreeing are profoundly challenging. Just think of the perverseness of it all: If you are single and want a child, you can have one. If you are married, and your husband doesn't want a child, you can't have one. If you live with someone who is a child, that doesn't count. You can't just adopt him and raise him right.

That, come to think of it, gets us to the heart of my household management problems with Stroller. They weren't really about taste. When we ventured out to go shopping together, we found we were always in agreement about what not to buy. I kept an eye out for things that might work in his house. For instance, his living room (significantly) was nearly empty of furniture; for a long time there was room for only one person to sit comfortably in front of the fireplace. One week, years ago, I got extremely organized and took Polaroids of some arm chairs, some lighting, a couple of bedside tables, and maybe a few other things that caught my eye. It was easy to do. Don't forget, in those days decorating was what I thought about for a living. Stroller approved the lot. A few weeks later, a van pulled up the drive.

"Why is there a moving van in front of the house? Is someone moving in? Or out, perhaps?"

"That's a small van, Stroller. Actually I'd call it a delivery truck."

But when two men stepped down, hauled out a ramp, and began unloading furniture into the house, Stroller was apoplectic.

"What is all that stuff? Where is it going?"

"Furniture, Stroller. It's called furniture. You approved it all."

"Yes. The pictures you showed me were nice. I didn't think the furniture would be real."

I didn't bother to point out that most people *pay* for decorating advice. It was all a matter of disharmony: what I saw as minor, he saw as major. Any change I made seemed huge to him. Any change he made seemed small to me. I wanted the house to look like us, like *ours*. He wanted to remain an only child.

We had gone to see a couples' therapist about why I couldn't get over my anger, hurt, and disappointment about Stroller's inability to get divorced. Why did I care? He loved me; I loved him; we spent our free time together; we cooked together; we kept house together (his house); we traveled together; we danced together—why should a little technicality like divorce matter? Didn't I enter adulthood with Joni Mitchell explaining how it goes: "I don't need no piece of paper from the city hall . . ." Actually, it has come to my attention, she said "*we* don't need" and she was talking about getting married, not getting unmarried, but still, you get the drift.

The ambivalence made a big difference in the quality of our lives—in a thousand ways, Stroller was like a squid squirting clouds of noxious ink around himself to hide from me. When we would become close, he would back up—with a shove at me. If it bothered me, he told me it was just because I secretly wanted to lead the dance. Why couldn't I just ignore the marriage? Why couldn't I just laugh off the distance?

The therapist looked up from the family diagram she had been trying to construct while I was talking, her sheet of paper covered with bubbles surrounding peoples' names, piled against each other and splitting off, amoebalike, to the margins. She was dumbfounded.

"We don't have to think about this one too hard," she said. "Never mind the deep psychological roots here, never mind your confusion. This is pretty simple. Just use the 'man in the street' test."

I had never come across this psychiatric concept in all my years of Freudian analysis.

"You know. The man in the street. You go out and ask the man in the street, 'What do you think? What does this sound like, this situation: a guy is married to someone he has legally separated from. He is having an affair with someone else. He won't leave his wife. Is this a healthy situation? Is this normal?'"

I conceded the point; the man in the street wouldn't get it at all. My sister didn't even get it, and she was about as far up my street as anyone could get. As I tried to explain it all to the therapist—the custody, the taxes, the estate planning, the psychology—she waved her hand in front of me impatiently.

"Thousands of people get divorced, every day. Thousands of people overcome their deep psychological issues from childhood. Thousands of people get lawyers, reorganize their lives, work out a strategy for the children, and move on. You did."

Yes, but I was, well, normal. At least, more normal. At least, I had been normal, once.

"This situation with Stroller is not at all normal. Just ask the man in the street. Anyway, why don't you think you are worth the effort?"

I left the therapist's office convinced that I was clearly no longer fit to talk to the man in the street, much less have one in my life.

When I later found the notes from this meeting in my journal, I was jolted by the familiar ring. It seemed that I had been asked the same question for years—*Why aren't you worth the commitment?*—but I had not heard it. Or, at least, I hadn't answered it.

After a few years of spending weekends with Stroller at his house, I had rearranged as much of the furniture as was agreed upon; organized linen closets, kitchen pantries, and book-shelves; and cleaned everything. The stories I could tell. I felt like a marital archaeologist, piecing together clues about what had gone wrong. The answer was all around us. So many of my disputes with Stroller about changing the furniture and dishes and paint colors were simply my way of trying to elbow aside a marriage that was dead but not dead—is there a marital purga-tory? And why was I the one who seemed to be stuck in it? It was sad and exhausting. I couldn't even imagine how his wife felt—but then again, I didn't have to, because she had started phoning me at odd hours. She was a screamer.

One hot afternoon at Stroller's house, I was overcome by a yen for gardening. Weekends were the only time I had free, and I had been neglecting my own garden, as I wasn't home enough. I wanted to start a little bed at his house, and was eyeing a tiny piece of real estate outside the kitchen door—an empty plot, about two feet across and a foot wide, full of dirt and stones.

What would that be, two square feet? Mind you, this was out of several hundred acres. I had to ask Stroller's permission.

"Can we just pull up one of these flagstones here on the back porch? The bed you have is too small and squashed up against the house—the cement of the foundation leaches nutrients so the soil isn't good there; I can't do much with it. But it's so sunny and warm back here—the perfect place for a kitchen garden. I'd love to put in some basil, some thyme, rosemary, maybe some verbena. I could dry the leaves and make infusions in the winter. You would love those."

I thought it sounded charming.

"Are you kidding?" He eyed me with profound suspicion. "The answer is *no*. Give you a foot, you'll want an acre."

It took me a couple of months to recover from that remark; I'm sure we broke up again. Looking back on it, the fight strikes me as a perfect summary of what kept going wrong between us: Stroller was afraid of giving anyone that acre, and I wanted it. The whole thing, and more. As soon as we made a step toward deepening our attachment—a long, peaceful, loving weekend, for instance, with no upset—Stroller would do something to push me away from him, and, in case I hadn't gotten far enough away, he would withdraw, refusing to speak to me, not answering the phone. Stroller wanted me fenced in, in my own pasture, just as he was tucked securely in his. I wanted limitless blue sky. One of us had to give up.

Well, after that fight over two square feet, the seasons rolled around, as they tended to do, and with spring, so had I, as I tended to do. Back at Stroller's house, time hung heavy on my hands; another year of those Saturdays of not being able to garden at my own house (if I wanted to see Stroller) were making me crazy to get into the soil. One day I saw some small pots of mint at the farmers' market. The farmer assured me the mint was strong enough to withstand the brutal country winters, and it didn't need room or good soil. I brought a few pots to Stroller's house and assured him that I was going to remain strictly within the existing boundaries. Which I did.

The mint did not.

To be honest, in those days I didn't realize how prolific mint could be, especially if it was in stony, dry soil where nothing else would thrive. From what I could see, the worse the conditions, the happier the mint. To be super honest, I forgot the fact that it was considered invasive. And to be absolutely truthful, I subconsciously wanted to unleash in his bed something that would never stay within its borders, no matter how much it was pushed back, cut down, and abused.

Within weeks, the mint took over the couple of feet it had been allotted. By the middle of summer, it had spread tendrils under the neighboring flagstones and begun to pop up on the other side of the terrace. It was positively biblical in its colonizing greed. And it was gorgeous stuff—its stiff, ridged leaves a deep, cool green. Aesthetically, I could have argued in defense of the plant that its presence softened the severe stone lines of that terrace. As an added bonus, whenever you went down the stairs and your foot brushed against the top of the mint, a wonderful fragrance wafted into the air.

Well, if my foot was brushing against the tops, that was only because Stroller was taking a machete to it every week.

As I had promised, in the autumn, I harvested mint leaves and dried them on screens; all winter, I brewed them with ginger, honey, and verbena. Delicious, healthy. Stroller drank it merrily. At bedtime, I put a sprig of mint into a glass of ice water, and he enjoyed it. The mint had a lot going for it. The next spring, many generations of mint appeared, prospered, and multiplied.

You can imagine my surprise when I arrived one late summer day to find nothing but the charred remains of mint, a crisp black ribbon across the back of the terrace.

"Oh yeah," Stroller said. "I had the lawn guy spray it with chemicals. That stuff is invasive."

"You just want to get rid of me! It's symbolic."

"No. I just want to be able to walk out the back door. I left ninety percent of the mint against the house."

"No you didn't. Not even ten percent."

"We'll compromise. Eighty-seven percent."

And that was the end of making new beds at Stroller's house. From then on, I stayed out of his garden.

You can now understand why I would start an invasion of mint across the lawn of my new house.

Just because I can. Because it is all mine.

14. COOKING FOR ONE

"HEY! WHAT ARE you doing there?"

I am at the small general store in the center of town, taking a break from unpacking boxes and weeding and typing, when I see my new neighbor, Perky.

"It's a job." Perky is behind the counter, at the cash register. "I never want to manage anyone else again. I'm alone now. I'm single. For the first time in my life."

I'm surprised by the frankness of her reply, given that I hardly know her, and, well, there are people around. I'm used to everyone in this town being so reserved that I don't find out their names, much less their marital status, until I read about them in the paper: the old birth, wedding, and death routine. I can't tell exactly how old she is—somewhere in her forties, if I had to guess. I can tell she is going to be a friend, so I decide to go out on a limb.

"I've been living on my own for fifteen years now," I tell her. "I mean, sort of on my own. Never mind. You'll get used to it. It isn't so bad."

"Oh, I'm not afraid or anything. The hardest thing is figuring out what to eat. I mean, I don't want to have cheese and crackers for dinner every night for the rest of my life."

I look around. We are standing in a grocery store. Dinner is all around us. Right behind me is breakfast, and next to that are four shelves groaning with snacks for bingeing on in front of the television. What is it about single women and food? But I know what she means. It has nothing to do with what's available—in fact, it has to do with what isn't available: food as a way to bond with someone else, whether a partner, a friend, a parent, or a child. This is, in fact, much on my mind as I am settling into my new house. Alone.

One way to look at this subject is to change it. Let's talk about single men and food. It will be a short conversation. When I was in my twenties, I asked my father, who was in one of his complaining modes about marriage, why he didn't just go live on his own.

"What? What would I do about dinner? Eat alone every night?"

Well, yes. Of course, what he really meant was that he still loved my mother.

The difference between men and women is that men last about three weeks on their own before they find someone else to do the cooking, whereas women—well, let me pluck another leaf from the Kentucky family tree. My aunt Kathleen was widowed in her forties. She didn't remarry for many years. In her seventies she fell in love; no one was more surprised than she. Events rolled along rapidly, as well they should at that age. She got married. Her new husband moved into her home, because, as she explained, he didn't have a home, just a house. He was a much older fellow, and in bad health; he died a few years later. She didn't seem devastated by this turn of events. Curious, I asked her if she had liked sharing her home with someone else after living alone for so many years. (I was being nosy, but after all, we are supposed to look to our elders for wisdom.)

"Honey, I didn't like it at all. I was used to doing things my way. I was used to having my rooms all to myself. And the snoring. You know. But the worst part of it was the meals. Every single day. As soon as one was done, another came along. What a bother. Men have to eat. You know how they are, sugar. They're not like us. I had forgotten how much cooking there is in a marriage. All those meals. All that cooking."

Yes, there's a lot of cooking in a marriage. And in raising children. There's a lot of cooking for holidays, and on vacations. There's cooking if you've been at the office all day. There's cooking if you've spent the day in a canoe. There's cooking if you've spent the day in the hospital, giving birth to another child, for whom there will be more cooking. Even in the course of the most passionate love affair, the kind when no one has time to eat a meal, much less prepare it, there will come a day when cooking has to happen, because no one wants to go out every night—and even if they did, it would be wrong, though for the life of me I cannot understand why. All those meals. All that cooking.

If you happen to be one of the women whose husbands do the cooking (as I was), don't think you're getting away with anything. It seems like you've lucked out, but you're going to pay for it. Don't go waving feminism in my face. You will become painfully aware, every time you lift a fork to your mouth, that the natural order of things has been upended, and that in some subtle way you have not triumphed as a feminist, but failed in the feminine. You will become aware that a halo of superiority has blossomed around your husband's head and that you are judged severely. You will also realize that you have gained twenty pounds since the wedding. And so has he. All those meals. All that cooking.

After my husband and I divorced, I had to start cooking, if only because I had two small boys to feed half of every week. Not one to keep things simple when complications are so close at hand, I served cheese soufflé every Tuesday for months, until the boys announced that they had become lactose intolerant. Then they became weary of popovers with peanut butter (protein!). I had mastered a roast chicken dish, but when my children rolled their eyes the hundredth time we had it, I lost the hang of making it. We switched to shrimp bisque, but peeling shrimp gave me nightmares of the heads crawling out of the trash, looking for revenge.

So, under the guise of teaching my children to develop proper restaurant voices and to place their napkins in their laps before eating, we became regulars at the local pizzeria. As a result, my sons are scarred for life by the mortification of dining with a woman who will send a dish back when it isn't prepared properly. Okay, I admit it: I'm the kind of person who would send a Happy Meal back at McDonald's. I thought I was teaching the children about standards, and the value of getting what you pay for, no matter where you are. Instead I was afflicting them with lifetime neuroses.

Eventually, the children left home, and, being single, I was forced to contemplate a lifetime of cooking for one. Or to remarry. I've always had a hard time cooking for myself, and for anyone else. Basically, I don't like it, especially if it involves meat. Within three days of living on my own for the first time, as a student in Paris, I became a vegetarian. It wasn't the carcasses stinking in the hot sun and dangling from enormous hooks under the awnings of the food stalls lining the streets around me. I was, after all, a doctor's daughter, and the sight of blood and guts didn't disturb me. The problem was touching it. Handling it. Getting it to the oven. Look, I wasn't the doctor.

By the time I've gotten through all the preparations for cooking—the scrubbing and scraping and grating and chopping and rubbing and coating and whatever else is required—I feel like I've been playing with my food for an hour. I'm tired of it. I've lost my appetite. And I find it appalling to see all my hard work, sometimes hours of it, disappear down people's throats in two minutes. This is why the greatest gift you can give a hostess is to eat slowly, with many exclamations of delight.

We live in a time of overheated enthusiasm for cooking, and someone has to stand up for the slackers among us. I'm delighted that there are so many wonderful cooks around; some of them are my very best friends. They're the people I can call when I'm feeling especially hungry for company and nurturance, and they're the ones who always welcome me to their tables. Nowadays, I try to show up with a batch of cookies. One of my friends is delighted to bring her skills to my house; when we shop and chop together, I remember how much fun that can be. In fact, in an unregenerate, unapologetic, un-PC, '50s-type of way, I desperately wish I had a wife. By now, I would even settle for being a wife, at pay grade. I am literally in awe of insouciance at the stove, because I'm the kind of person who quails before a cookbook. I'm intimidated. Things never seem to turn out the way they are supposed to, and I usually can't figure out why. Even frozen ravioli is a calamity; the pockets break open, and weird bits of innards bubble to the top, or, worse, they all stick together in a congealed mass, as happened just the other night.

I have a hard time following directions, which makes recipes tedious. And I'm very sensitive to know-it-alls, many of whom, appropriately enough, are cookbook writers. My habits of skipping ingredients, confusing tsp with tbsp (see how easy that is?), or, worse, what I call my tendency toward muchness—You like raisins? Why not triple what the recipe calls for?—these quirks don't help matters. I even get deadline stress while preheating.

The problem is, I love to eat. And I love to drink. I love whiskey and scotch and fine wines. But not alone. And I have a china fetish, by which I mean I love to set a beautiful table. So I'm at cross-purposes with myself, always looking for the next fabulous dinner. Since I normally don't cook myself a meal, I'll usually eat granola, yogurt, or—yes, there it is, the dreaded cheese and crackers—some variation on the contents of the single woman's pantry. I am a creature of habit. I don't mind eating the same thing over and over. I love not having to reinvent the wheel every day. Yet there comes a time when even I am unable to pour myself another bowl of Grape-Nuts, no matter how lovely the bowl is.

If I could muster the will to cook, I would have time for a new experience: having friends over for dinner. I could organize a mental health safety network: a whole season ahead of houseguests. The thought makes me groan. My friend Abby, who lives nearby, tells me that all I need to have under control is three or four meals to entertain to my heart's content. Then again, she's an artist. Creativity at the end of a handle attached to a paintbrush or a spoon is no big deal for her. My friend Caroline decides that one of her life goals is to get me over my cooking inhibitions, in three months. She may be able to do it, as I like nothing more than her Brussels sprouts with bacon and mustard seeds, or the cabbage dish she always prepares. But when I watch her pounding and smacking and hitting the chicken for paillard, I have to wonder, What is going on here? What's with the enthusiasm for hitting a dead thing? However, if anyone can help you get over your troubles, whether in the kitchen or the bedroom or the boardroom, it is your friends. So I am paying more attention to their lessons, launching myself into their courses of self-improvement.

I am beginning to think that I have the wrong perspective on cooking for myself. A delicious underbelly to the problem is presenting itself: I am free. I am unfettered. I can be as demanding, forgiving, creative, or boring about what and when and how I eat. I can skip meals. Or I can eat three meals at once.

Here is the good news about cooking for one: shopping for one. You will never again have to set foot in a Price Club, Costco, Walmart, or Sam's Club. Not for you, those groaning shelves loaded with five-pound boxes of cereal, twelve-gallon bottles of orange juice, and packages of thirty-four rolls of toilet paper. They were probably never for you in the first place, unless you were running a restaurant. Those places are temples to the marketing gods, who have tricked an entire population of otherwise rational people into thinking they are saving money when they buy in bulk. By the time your average family household of 3.2 gets halfway through that ten-pound bag of basmati rice, they're sharing it with an extended family of mice. The other good news about cooking for one is that even though organic food is more expensive, you have to buy so little of it that it is affordable. You can practice *ecosattva*, a term I recently picked up that has something to do with being kind to the planet.

Let us remind ourselves that shopping is not about need. Yes, you need to eat. But if that's all there were to it, you could get in and out of the market in three minutes flat. It would probably be better for all of us to eat pretty much the same small quantities, day in and day out. But shopping for food, like shopping for shoes, is about fantasy, hope, dreams, and the expectation that the right purchase will lead to living happily ever after.

I cannot get out of supermarkets in less than half an hour, no matter what I do. I find them exhilarating, fascinating, and reassuring places. First of all, the plenitude: the mind-boggling array of food. I know it is proper nowadays, a habit of the weary environmentalist, to cluck about how depleted our food stock has become, how there used to be fifty-eight varieties of apple available to feeders (that would be us). I am of the opinion that it is amazing, and nearly paralyzing, to have a mere ten varieties from which to choose. How is anyone supposed to remember that Pink Ladies are the ones you don't like?

When you visit the typical suburban-style American supermarket, overheated from the effort of finding a parking space, you can linger in what used to be the vegetable aisle but is now a miniature rain forest, and wait for the rainy season, which arrives every three minutes or so, and listen to the water drip gently over the crisp arugula, the watercress, the mint, the basil, the fennel, the sage, and feel the cool mist across your arms, and even get a little hit of aromatherapy and moisturizing.

In the face of supermarket plenitude, shopping for one gets dicey. Everything at what used to be the regular supermarket has gotten bigger too: the store, first of all, and the aisles, the carts, the variety, and most significantly, the portions. It is literally impossible to buy a package of chicken for one. And just try breaking apart a block of frozen asparagus so that you don't have to eat the wretched leftover spears for three days. Soup, you would think, is a safe bet. But if you make your own, prepare to eat lentil soup for the next six days, as there is no such thing as preparing a single dinner portion of appetizing, hearty soup.

They (the wise ones with gurus) say that intention is everything. So with all good intentions of learning to cook for myself, I decide to try my hand at Brussels sprouts. I'm aware that I have a habit of buying too much; though Caroline's recipe calls for three pints of sprouts, I'm cooking for one. So I stand in front of the overflowing bin trying to remember how many of those things were on my plate last time I had them at a restaurant. Eight? I put eight in a plastic bag, but they look ridiculous. Why go to all the trouble of preparing only eight sprouts? So

I add eight more, and then a few more, and before I know it, I have enough Brussels sprouts for a family of four. Then I have to buy a jar of mustard seeds, and then another jar of mustard with seeds, and then olive oil, as I'm not sure whether what I have is rancid after all these years. Before I know it, my dish of Brussels sprouts is about to cost me about twenty dollars. I would have been safer in the prepared foods section. But then I wouldn't have been cooking for myself, would I? I resign myself to five days of Brussels sprouts, a shame, really, when I consider how much Stroller had loved Brussels sprouts, and how he had always ordered them when they were on the menu. If we were together, there would never be too many Brussels sprouts.

Because you are shopping alone, and only for yourself, you have exclusive rights to the special pleasure of letting go of time, and losing, or finding, yourself in a reverie. This doesn't make shopping efficient, but it does make it fun. They aren't the most romantic of places, but to my mind supermarkets are underrated for their Proustian heft.

My shopping style might be problematic for others, but it works for me. I learned from a master. My father is the sort of person who cannot be trusted on his own with a grocery list. Therefore, when I was a child, he was always my favorite person to shop with, though it was a rare occasion. None of this "We're not spending money on that" or "Put that back where you found it" or "You'll never eat that" or, the worst, "That's not on the list." That was my mother, who certainly knew how to keep a strict budget. In fact, I grew up thinking that the only clothes anyone was ever allowed to buy were the ones on racks marked SALE; the other ones, according to my mother, were for display only, to show you what would eventually be for sale. I was out of college before I had the temerity to approach the full-price racks. Thrift was bred into me, and guilt still attends every purchase I make.

My father was the same sort of shopper no matter where he was, lavish, charming, haphazard, and it drove my mother crazy. In defiance, my father became secretive about his shopping. Over the years, I have acquired from him a sizable collection of Don't Tell Your Mother gifts: a Don't Tell Your Mother barbecue grill, the Don't Tell Your Mother recordings of the Bach cantatas, a Don't Tell Your Mother wheelbarrow. My children's bank accounts were sometimes increased with Don't Tell Your Mother money. I grew up having an endless Don't Tell Your Mother conversation with him about my mother, about his own ambivalence and sorrow in his life, so unresolved, so poignant, so frustrating in its intractable pain that it threaded its way into my dreams and lay coiled in the depths of any love I was ever to feel for another man. Which may, in fact, begin to explain my attachment to Stroller.

For my father, a shopping list was, if not meaningless, just the beginning. It is from him that I picked up my zigzag technique of shopping. And in this, as in all things, the world divides into two types: those who efficiently and swiftly make only the stops on the list, and those who must stop to check everything out, no matter how long it takes. My father and I always began at the left side of the store, with me pushing the cart, and an hour and two carts later, the right side would appear over the horizon.

However, we never spent much time in the meat section. I tried to steer clear of it, and it didn't seem to hold any fascination for him, perhaps because as a surgeon he'd spent the day at an operating table with open bodies. My father had an exacting expectation of how his girls would turn out, and it was frequently articulated at dinner, which, after all, would be the only time in the day we would have seen him.

"Do you know what human fat looks like, girls?" my father would say as we were cutting into our roast beef.

"No, Daddy."

"It is disgusting. I did a six-hour operation today, and it could have been a three-hour operation, but this patient was very, very fat. Look at the fat at the edge of your meat." We would gaze down at our plates, heads hung in shame that we were anywhere near fat. "Fat is yellow, jiggly, slippery. You can't get to the important stuff without cutting through the fat. It is hard to control. Your knife slides in it. It slips out of the clamps. Do you want to be covered with fat like that, girls?"

By this time, my sisters, in tears, would put down their knives and forks, only to pilfer boxes of cookies after bedtime. I found this all fascinating, in a dreadful way, and would meticulously trim my way through the meat to prove that I was ready for medical school, eating at least three helpings, my metabolism haywire with anxiety.

My father's particular supermarket Charybdis was the frozen foods section, specifically, the coast of Sara Lee. I can never see a box of frozen Chocolate Fudge Cake without thinking of shopping with him, and I still find myself lingering there from time to time, pulling my sweater tight for warmth, remembering.

More than remembering. Activating purchase power. The best things about shopping for one? You can indulge in *ego*sattva: kindness to yourself. You can buy all the Sara Lee frozen Chocolate Fudge Cake you want, and there's no one around to remind you of a budget.

15. MUFFINS

WHILE ORGANIZING MY cozy kitchen in Rhode Island, getting rid of every cracked, dirty, and redundant item (most things), I have an epiphany about my cooking problems. Why am I fighting my true nature? Why am I tempting the fates by looking at recipes that call for minutely calibrated ingredients, recipes so finely tuned that if one thing is off, the entire dish is a disaster? Do I ever need to eat braised beef cheeks and veal tongue with baby leeks and horseradish cream? Instead of recipes that are the cooking equivalent of a Porsche, what I need is the equivalent of the kind of car I love to drive—the station wagon. Meals with wheels. Meals that can handle cargo: lots of simple ingredients.

Being something of a car nut, I've driven every kind of car there is. I've driven high-powered sports cars—my father's turquoise Oldsmobile from the late '60s is forever imprinted upon my soul as the dream vehicle. But I've never owned a racy little automobile. I have come to dislike anything that demands constant attention, whether it is dogs, dishwashers, or, finally, men. I like things that are independent, and that need you only because they want you, not because they'll have a breakdown without you. I've driven sedans, VW buses, coupes, hatchbacks, convertibles, and yes, even SUVs. But my favorite car by far is my station wagon. It is sturdy, reliable, low-maintenance, carries a lot of baggage, and always gets me where I want to go, with minimum fuss and bother.

I've been told that the inside of my car looks like it belongs to a teenage boy, so I may also be living out some sort of cross-dressed Peter Pan fantasy. I've given up trying to keep my station wagon free of sand and dirt; I make too many trips to the nursery and to the beach, coming back loaded with plants, bags of compost, sandy towels, and wet bathing suits. The car is, literally, dirty. Not full of trash, as I like to keep it clear of water bottles and Kleenex, but soil. I don't worry about it anymore. In fact—and this is thanks to Stroller, who was proud of letting things get wear and tear and went out of his way to rough them up—I feel liberated from the vacuum cleaner and the whisk broom, and freely throw anything I please into the back. I keep a basket there that always holds: a flashlight; patching spray for punctured tires (another gift from Stroller, who believed in being prepared for life's inevitable breakdowns, at which he is practiced); maps; a magnifying glass (so I can actually read the maps); string bags for the grocery store (someday I'll actually remember to take them into the grocery store when I'm shopping); a trowel and garden clippers for those many times I see something along the side of the road that I cannot resist; a couple of umbrellas (hoping for company on a rainy detour); a few rocks, shells, and bits of sea glass from the beach (my car collection); a bathing suit (you never know); flip-flops (same); sneakers (for when I might be stranded somewhere and have to walk five miles for help); straps (for my son's surfboard); and a baggie full of loose change (for those coffee cans at the farm stands). As I describe this inventory, I see that I am also living out a Girl Scout fantasy, awarding myself merit badges, so to speak, every time I successfully transport and transplant a flower from someone else's garden into mine, or navigate—without GPS, which is for sissies—the back roads in the dark to a restaurant in some godforsaken country town.

It occurs to me, one morning when I get up hungry for something other than my usual boiled egg, that I need to think of my cooking style as more like my driving style. That's when I begin to bake muffins. Not just any old kind of muffin, but the kind that represented hippie living at its finest when I was a teenager in the '70s: the bran muffin. Once artisanal goods, muffins have gone the way of breads; in the last decade they have been mass-produced in factories and shipped out to stores for a final heating, their ingredients aimed at the lowest common denominator of taste. How else can you explain why a so-called homemade muffin from a market in Texas tastes exactly the same as one from that shop in Massachusetts? The other salient feature of store-bought muffins is that they are now typically the size of a child's head, which can also be said of store-bought cookies. This is not a change for the better, as it means you have to fight with yourself about your lack of discipline in eating the equivalent of three cookies in one round, which spoils the fun of a cookie. I'm especially bitter about what has happened to store-bought bran muffins, as they no longer pack any punch, except for the occasional bite that contains a razor-sharp shard of bran—or perhaps packing material. Toothsome, I believe, describes what I am looking for in my bran muffin.

After a quick troll through a few recipe websites online, I realize that while the supermarket muffin has become a boring facsimile of itself, the real home-cooked bran muffin has evolved mightily in the last three decades. It has become a station wagon of the food world: it's good for you and able to carry many things reliably, with a minimum of fuss. And, to top it off, an hour in the kitchen, using only basic tools (spoons and bowls, not even a mixer), yields enough to last a couple of weeks, if you play your freezer space right.

When I try a basic bran flax muffin recipe from a site called allrecipes.com, I judge it to be wanting. It has some of the ingredients I like—such as coconut and carrots—but it is missing others, such as raisins and nuts. By the way, that is the only trustworthy method for choosing a recipe of any sort: if it has the ingredients you like, you will enjoy the combination of them. If some of them are suspect, they will only be made worse in the aggregate. This is true of muffins, and of men, come to think of it. Bad ingredients don't get folded into the batter; they are mysteriously enhanced in the combining.

I search around allrecipes.com a bit longer, and that is when I discover the section below the recipe for users' reviews, a veritable Talmud of cooking. There are hundreds of reviews for the bran muffin recipes. And that is how I wake to my new-found affinity for vehicular recipes, foods that carry many foods within them. "This recipe is a great way to have veggies and fruit in the morning," writes DAVIST, who then describes several alterations to the recipe. I try them. TUNISIANSWIFE writes, "A great recipe to help clean out the refrigerator crisper," and then describes her variations on the theme. I try those, too.

I feel like I have stumbled upon my long-lost tribe. Clearly, bran muffins are inspiring paroxysms of passion among them. I can relate to this; these are my people. I soon learn to go straight to the modifications as soon as I spot an appealing recipe. Before too long, the bran muffin has transmogrified into the Morning Glory, and from there I start on savory muffins, full of bacon and cheese. I am in a paradise of "embroidering on wishes"—that's what people do who always give you much more than what you asked for. If you wish for a room painted white, you will get an extra few stripes of red. If you wish for a knitted scarf, you might get one covered with seed pearls and feathers, too. Some cooks want the muffins to be made with a different kind of sugar, and more of it; others obsess about the kind of oil or flour called for, describing alternatives using whole wheat or spelt, whatever that is. People post photographs of their muffins. DETECTIVEL from Toronto added oat flakes to the tops, no doubt dressing them up for the photo shoot. CHRISTINE M gathered hers into a straw basket and placed it on a lacy tablecloth, which derailed me for a day or two as I pondered the virtues of lace and scoured the Internet for inexpensive sources of eyelet—until I realized I was simply wallowing in nostalgia for my older son's infant love object, Froggie Woggie, who had been edged in eyelet. I returned to muffins.

People also post pictures of themselves and share their cooking proficiency. They post commentary from Australia, Nova Scotia, Alaska, North Carolina, and they give themselves rabbinical names, such as WILDOREGANO, GLOWWORM, CHEEZY-GIRL, and CUPSPINNER. I spend a while contemplating the image of PACHA in Ottawa, elegant and mysterious, seated against the balustrade of a balcony, her long blond hair in two braids, a gorgeous Victorian building looming behind her. Is that the view from her kitchen window? Who wears braids anymore? Why don't I live in Ottawa, if it looks like that?

Suddenly I find myself in the company of hundreds of women, cooking and kibitzing. It is just like being at the office, only better. If I don't feel like it, I don't have to talk to anyone, or worry about anyone, or fire anyone. The women online share bits of their lives, too: some are pregnant, some make muffins for their dogs or rabbits, some bring the muffins to colleagues at the office, some feed them to their kids, who scarf them down, or to their husbands, who complain about the carrots. During my muffin era, I never feel alone and helpless in the kitchen. No matter what hour of the day or night, there is someone—there are hundreds—able and willing to help me figure out what to do, to console and commiserate. It is one gigantic, glorious eavesdrop. I get to the point where I am looking for muffin recipes in obscure corners of the web late at night, and forgetting to take note of where I've been, so that by morning the muffins are gone, like a dream, eloquent about my desires, but never to be recovered.

I am a compulsively neat cook. It is my way of maintaining order and control over my environment, and it symbolizes my need to maintain order and control over everything when I know I have no control over anything, and the universe is not an orderly place. Be that as it may, I think the world divides into two schools of thought on this issue: one equates messy cooking with professionalism—it implies knowing that the staff, or your wife, will clean up after you—and yes, most men are terribly messy cooks; the other equates messy cooking with making a mess. I am of the latter frame of mind. I can afford to be, as I don't cook often, nor do I undertake anything too elaborate. Housekeeping gives me the same comfort I got from having a job: there is a proper order to things, there is routine, there are no existential dilemmas (you don't question why, you just do it), and the work is never done.

I clean as I go. First, I take down all the ingredients I will need and display them on the counter, as if they were in a store, or on a TV show. I find this makes me feel proud and serious in my intention to do a good job. Anyone with even a smidgen of spirituality will tell you that intentions are critical. If it's a really slow day, I style my ingredients, so to speak, hours ahead of time, arranging the boxes according to height, balancing the color palette, so that I have plenty of time to admire the scenario and anticipate my chores. Otherwise, the experience goes by so quickly it seems worthless to have begun.

You must take pride in your tools. When you realize your sifter is rusty from that time you mistakenly let it soak for a few days before cleaning it, you must throw the sifter away and buy a new one, even if it means you have to wait a few days to go back to cooking. Otherwise, you will always convince yourself that you will do it next time. Lay the tools out before you the way a surgeon, or rather—again, two schools—his nurse, would do before an operation. Sharpen the knives, wipe out the bowls, organize the measuring cups. Do anything, in short, to heighten the ceremonial quality of your endeavor.

I like to put a box away after I have added an ingredient. This is a crutch I have developed to compensate for my absentmindedness. If the flour is back on the shelf, that means it has been used already and you won't be in danger of adding it twice—unless, of course, you forget to take it off the shelf in the first place, but I can't come up with a safety net for everything. That's why you spend hours preparing, so that you notice if you have forgotten something basic. And make sure to screw the lids of the spice jars on tight. You don't think anyone needs such elementary advice? I wish someone had warned me before the lid of the cinnamon jar fell off in my spice rack and left a light, fragrant dusting over the contents of my pantry.

I add ingredients in well-shaped lumps and I never stir until everything is in. That way, I can go back and count the number of teaspoons of cinnamon I have added if I lose track, because there they are: three little heaps. I wonder why they don't make the openings to spice jars large enough for a teaspoon, though. I also choose recipes that are not overly sensitive to confusions between tsp and Tbsp. My other problems cluster around definitions of terms, such as *grating* and *shredding*. During my first pass at a variation on bran muffins, I gave up shredding the carrots on the cheese grater when I no longer had a thumbnail and found myself considering the nutritional content of blood. Frances came to the rescue when she suggested I buy a tiny food processor, the kind you use to make baby food. It shreds, grates, pulverizes, juliennes, and otherwise processes anything you want. And it doesn't make you feel bad that you are single.

Muffins are only one of my favorite station-wagon foods. They are forgiving and they carry their weight. The vehicular epiphany has opened me up to a vast universe of other station-wagon recipes: pastas and risottos of all sorts, and even—yes, if I can make them, you can too—soufflés. My favorite recipe by far is for a mulligatawny soup from *The Fannie Farmer Cookbook*, but I've changed a few things. These kinds of dishes respond well to cooking by feel; for instance, you can tell, once you get the basics down, what sort of ratio of dry to wet ingredients you need to keep things together.

In honor of my new desire to learn to cook, Alex and my parents present me with a slow cooker for Christmas. They seem to be on to something; it is just my speed. I have a faint but fond memory of them from the '70s, the heyday of Crock-Pots. All these years later, my son is the one who has become obsessed with them. Alex, living on his own, has become adept at slow cooking for one: he makes stews and soups on the weekends and freezes portions to eat through the week. He amazes me. I let my cooker marinate in its box for a few months, until curiosity gets the better of me and I unpack it and get to work. I see the light pretty quickly. What's not to love about an appliance you can throw things into in the morning, leave, and find waiting for you in the evening with something more delectable, fragrant, and tasty inside than when you left it? Food snobs—and they come out of the woodwork the minute you start raving about slow cookers—will tell you that you're simply braising, and that special equipment is not necessary. They may be right on a technicality, but they're wrong in spirit. The operative word is *special*, as in equipment that gives you confidence. The key thing about a slow cooker is that once everything goes in, you simply are not allowed to open the lid. You do not want the magic to escape. It quickly becomes apparent that it is impossible even for me to screw up slow-cooker recipes.

But the most wonderful thing about slow cooking is that it gives you the gift of time. It bestows a gentle, heartening halo of feeling that everything is, or will soon be, under control, and you can become insouciant, one of the desirable states of human evolution. While you are preparing dinner for ten, you can leave the house; you can go to a yoga class and not panic upon awakening from a two-hour corpse pose; you can knit several more inches of scarf; you can practice a Haydn piano sonata; you can organize your linen closet; you can weed the garden. You can do all these things—and still be cooking.

The slow cooker solves a lot of problems, not least among them the clean-up issue. There's nothing like being able to serve a hearty dinner for twelve friends in an immaculate kitchen, because you've had plenty of time to wash the dishes while the cooking just happened on its own. Needless to say, slow cooking quickly becomes a happy part of falling in slow love. It has given me the confidence to throw a dinner party.

While I am in the middle of experimenting with a risotto one evening, my architect friend Dan calls. He is of Romanian origin, so I always have to follow his language carefully. He's been ill, so I ask him how he is feeling. "Much better a little bit," he says. And it strikes me, as I stir the risotto, that his reply makes perfect sense, and describes not only the way small changes can make big differences (using coconut instead of carrots, for instance), but also the way even the smallest improvements can have an enormous effect in certain contexts. Sit down and slowly, deliberately, thoughtfully eat your risotto full of peas and sausage, or your muffin full of apples and raisins, and you will see what I mean, especially if it is 4:00 A.M.

And, by the way, I ought to mention that you should take care to organize your music before you start pouring and mixing. Yes, your life has a sound track—or it should. The music will make its way into the food. Take advantage of living alone. Play music in the middle of the night, if that's when you feel like cooking, and crank it up as loud as you want. Who is going to complain? Put on those Bach Cello Suites and believe that you, too, will once again have a passionate love affair. Load up Al Green and believe in sex after fifty. Listen to Alison Krauss tell you about that "restless feeling knocking at my door today." Pay attention when Emmylou Harris tells you "some say love is like smoke beyond all repair"—that's such a good line that I scribbled it in chalk on my hearth. Of course love is like smoke. That is why you are alone in the kitchen at 2:00 A.M, is it not? Just try not to burn the muffins.

Summer

THE USES OF SORROW

(In my sleep I dreamed this poem)

Someone I loved once gave me
a box full of darkness.

It took me years to understand
that this, too, was a gift.

—MARY OLIVER

16. THE DIET

A DMITTEDLY, THERE COMES a time of too many muffins. Everything, it seems, can be turned into a muffin. You find yourself wondering why there can't be chicken muffins, or salmon muffins, or meat muffins, forgetting for a moment, that these do exist, and they are called burgers. And then you begin to feel sluggish, craving the constant fuel injection of sugar. You pine for past decades, when a day or two of skipping meals was all it took to restore youth and vitality. You begin to fret about losing a hefty investment in the wardrobe market, because nothing fits anymore. You begin to ponder elasticized waistbands, for heaven's sake, and linen shifts, because linen is forgiving: even skin doesn't wrinkle as badly as linen. You even begin to talk about "the end of sex"; how could anyone else bear to look at your body in this condition? You feel terribly out of control. And yet, you can't stop baking muffins. Where else can you find such reliable comfort?

One day, I take myself to the gynecologist for my annual physical exam. I'm dreading the visit. Dr. Pat is a formidable lady, and I use the term advisedly. She is glamorous and brilliant and she swears like a trucker. She is also five feet two and cannot weigh more than a hundred pounds. Or, to put it another way, she wears size 0 clothing, made in a parallel universe as a disguise for alien visitors to what is shaping up to be my new size 10 planet.

My doctor works like a demon. I have never met anyone so devoted to her practice. She maintains strict standards for herself, for her office, and for her patients. Her standards know no bounds. The first thing she checks during the examination is your underwear: what kind are you wearing, and what shape is it in? Many an unsuspecting patient has been chewed out for substandard issue.

"What on earth do you call those things you are wearing? Don't give me comfortable. You expect your husband/boyfriend/emergency room doctor to respect you in those? Or want to have sex with you? Have you given up on life?"

Dr. Pat is an unregenerate flirt. She loves men. And she knows how to deal with them, too. My sister and I took her to the opera one evening, and she arrived straight from the office twinkling with rhinestones. A grumpy elderly man was blocking us from our seats; reluctantly, muttering, he got up to let us pass. We settled in, and moments later, Pat was flirting up a storm with our neighbor, who was soon ready to let her sit in his lap. We kidded her about her uncontrollable urge to flirt with anyone. "I know," she said, sighing wistfully. "I could flirt with a lamppost." She writes blogs about "cougars and crones," calling on women over forty to shed the wizened, docile image of old age and get in touch with their inner cat. She gives advice to her patients on how to improve their sex lives, and how to talk to their partners about difficult issues—only once during the weekend, and only after that special Saturday morning sex. ("Don't talk to me about errand day! Make time! Have you given up on life?" Dr. Pat loves life.)

Every woman needs a Dr. Pat on her side. Giving up on underwear is one of the first signs of giving up on life, and so I have purchased special lacy bikini underwear just for my visits to Dr. Pat, so that she will not give up on me.

After she has checked your underwear, the next thing she checks is your weight. All doctors check your weight and record it on those mysterious little charts, which, if you ever peek at them, are completely illegible—except for your weight! Dr. Pat is not the kind of doctor who notes the figure politely while remarking gently on the unending primary elections, the overheated weather, or your summer vacation. She is the kind of doctor (well, she's the only one of her kind that I know) who will actually make rude remarks about your weight. "Two pounds? You think that's nothing? Two pounds every year for ten years is twenty pounds, dear. If I'm doing the math correctly. And I think I am. After you're fifty, twenty pounds is like forty pounds. Out of control." And so on.

I met Dr. Pat for the first time two years before the magazine folded. During that first visit to her office (an appointment for which she had asked me to allot several hours), she laid out the principles on which her practice was built. She had grown up in a tiny town in Kentucky and been educated in a one-room schoolhouse—this was not a hundred years ago, but in the '50s! She wanted a practice that reflected the caring, intimacy, and nosiness of a close-knit community. This perhaps explains, or actually erases, the boundary issues, if you must call them that. She was raised in the kind of town where everything is everyone's business; nothing is off-limits. She expects her patients to tell her everything about themselves and their bodies, what happened to them, and what they have done with them. If you don't want that kind of doctor, she doesn't want you as a patient. That's why the first visit with her takes many hours.

The life of my body had been, to that point, remarkably unremarkable. I had never been in the hospital for an illness. I rarely took aspirin. I didn't drink to excess or smoke pot, as several of my friends suddenly seemed to be doing all over again—twice a day, even!—as they hit their fifties. I had given birth to two babies without any sort of pain control, though mainly because I waited too long before I began to beg for it. While I was telling Dr. Pat my medical history, I could see by the tiny frown between her eyes that it was not good enough, or bad enough. Surely there was something I was forgetting? Yes. Suddenly I remembered a "significant medical event" from my twenties. How could I have forgotten it?

I had awoken one morning with a mild backache (this was in Austin, Texas, where I had gone to work at a magazine). I attributed the discomfort to overdoing it in the swimming pool the day before, thinking it was probably just sunburn. By noon, I was in enough pain that I became convinced that the mattress in my rental was no good, so I talked my husband-to-be into driving to the mall for firmer bedding. My family is nothing if not well versed in the art of denial. Before the new mattress was delivered to our house, I was stricken with seizures so severe that I could no longer stand up. I was crouched on the living room floor, howling dementedly with the worst pain I had ever felt in my life. Within an hour, I developed a raging fever and became delirious. My husband-to-be looked on with pity and terror in his eyes, wondering, no doubt, if this was a foretaste of life with me.

All I remember after this point is that I became convinced that I had entered hell, that it was a real and terrible place, that I wanted the entire neighborhood to know that I was being possessed by demons who were carving tunnels through my back and fighting one another for possession of my soul. I had by then crawled across the floor to maneuver myself into the corner of the living room to block the devils' entry into my body—which was pointless, as everyone knows evil spirits think nothing of going right through walls. And they were! I could hear them! They were in the yard, gnawing through the back of the house to get into me, crunching through the wood. I was raving about all this to my quintessentially rational boyfriend, and it was at this point that he thought it might be time to get help.

Of course, by the time we got to the hospital, the kidney stone, which is what had possessed me, had done its damage and left behind a ragged trail.

I closed my recitation to Dr. Pat of this significant medical event with the prideful comment that the pain of delivering hefty baby boys did not come close to the pain I felt while passing kidney stones. (So, by the way, enough with the comments about men not understanding childbirth: just think how much farther their stones must travel on their arduous journey out.)

Dr. Pat was sitting up straighter, scribbling furiously. Finally, I was giving her some good material. "Was there a follow-up to this event? What? No one saw you again? Where was this? Texas?" Clearly, I had spent my late twenties in a backwater of America.

"Have you passed any more kidney stones?" I thought perhaps I might have, but nothing quite as severe, probably more like rocks instead of boulders. "Is someone monitoring your kidneys?"

By this time in my life I couldn't even remember where my kidneys were. So many other organs, like my expanding stomach and my swollen womb and my broken heart, had hove into view. I assured her that I had been free of kidney awareness for decades. But I left her office with a note to see a radiologist for a typical baseline vaginal ultrasound.

"And, while you're at it, get an abdominal scan. You might as well."

I put that appointment off for months: I had too much to do, too tight a schedule to satisfy someone's baseline curiosity. But Dr. Pat hounded me—she is indefatigable about patient care—and finally I lay down on the table and had my belly slathered with warm gel. I hadn't had an ultrasound since I had last been pregnant sixteen years earlier—how dear is the memory of the first sight of my tadpole of a son, his brain split in two, his heart thumping outside his body. Things had improved, technologically speaking. I lay on my back and asked the technician to swivel the screen so I could see it as he examined my insides.

"Tell me about all the organs, while you're going around," I said. "I can't remember a thing about my anatomy once you get past the uterus." That organ was fine. So were those eccentric-looking antlers of ovaries. He began ticking things off clockwise. "There's your bladder, looks perfect. There's your kidney, excellent."

I was shocked at how big the kidney was; somehow, I had confused kidneys with kidney beans. One was the size of a nickel, and the other the size of a fist. Well, that revelation alone was worth the price of admission, and I began to regret, for the millionth time, my decision not to go to medical school. Bodies are so fascinating and straightforward and, well, knowable.

"Your gallbladder is good   "

"Are you sure? I'm not so sure. Will you take another look? I seem to be unable to drink gin any longer. Or vodka. I can't remember which. One of those clear ones. Of course, you can't tell with martinis anymore, they make them out of anything. But after martinis I get terrible cramps. Awful. The kind that ruin the evening. I was thinking it might be a bad gallbladder."

Naturally, I had not mentioned this to Dr. Pat.

"Nope, gallbladder is fine. No sign of inflammation."

This guy could have told me the eye color of my unborn children. "You're a perfectly boring patient." He squished more warm gel on my belly and pressed round further down the other side, ticking off a couple more organs. I remembered what I learned in high school biology about symmetry.

The technician grew quiet. I figured he was bored; the left side just mirrors the right side, as I recalled. Soon, though, pictures were being frozen on the screen, which was now swiveled away from me, measurements were being taken, and other people called in to look. They were calm, scrutinizing the gray images on the screen, so I was only mildly curious, until a beautiful white-coated doctor looked me in the eye and said, gently, "Don't worry. I'm sure we're going to be treating you for a very long time. Dr. Pat would like you to call her. Immediately."

That clued me in.

In short, Dr. Pat told me that I was to cancel lunch and get to the hospital.

"But it's with my agent. Are you sure? That took forever to schedule."

"Honey, if it were my mass, I'd want to get it checked out as soon as possible."

"Mass? What's that?"

Dr. Pat sent me for a CAT scan and an MRI and anything else she and her colleagues could think of. I finally began to understand that I was in trouble when the doctors kept shoveling me, on my hard slab, into that tunnel over and over again for more pictures. It was freezing; I was trembling; my hand with a large needle in it was throbbing, as it had taken several stabs to find an actual blood supply. Tears began to leak out of my eyes and slide sideways down my face, pooling in my ears. All I could think of was, *Alex will be okay. He is sort of grown up. But Theo is still*

in high school. He still lives at home. He still lives with me. He is really
way too young for me to leave him. Please. Make this go away.

The radiologists refused to tell me what was going on. I
had to make another appointment with a different doctor. That
night, I waited until after the opera to tell Stroller about the
developments of the day. I had calmed down, and found refuge
in our family's favorite destination: the state of denial. I didn't
want to spoil the evening with something that would most
likely turn out to be a false alarm, or a little nothing. Stroller
instantly became kinder and more solicitous of me than he had
ever been; something about my leaving *this* life, as opposed to
his life (which he remained ambivalent about), moved him
profoundly.

I went to the surgeon's office alone the next day. I was still
confused as to what all the fuss was about, and I was sure it would
turn out to be insignificant. He was brisk, straightforward, and
clearly bored by my case. I began to wish I had paid attention to
the wisdom of never going to the doctor alone.

"I've done this operation thousands of times."

"What operation? Everyone keeps using these terms—
mass, *growth*. What are you talking about? "

The doctor, who was younger than I by several years (when
did that start to happen?), shrugged his shoulders.

"Mass. Growth. Tumor. It's all just words. It's all the same.
Cancer." He shrugged. "You have kidney cancer."

I decided on the spot that since he was supposed to be a
great surgeon, the only bedside manner I cared about would be
on display when I was unconscious.

To make a long story a bit shorter, within a couple of weeks I was on my back on what looked like a giant tea trolley, waving goodbye to Stroller and my family, being wheeled into the operating room to have my kidney removed. I put on a brave smile as they receded from view and I entered a busy, bright place. Dr. Pat stood at the end of the table, just behind my surgeon, and as the team of doctors introduced themselves, she squeezed my foot.

"See? I'm here. I told you I would be. I'm not going anywhere until you are out of here. And I'm wearing my good luck angel earrings. The gold ones."

Even in the OR, she was impossibly chic. My guardian angel.

I had known she would be there. I had had my hair done the day before—for her!—so that I wouldn't look the way I felt, and I hoped she noticed before it was all tucked into some sort of shower cap. I was also wearing the special underwear, but how could she have known? I smiled wanly at my failure to prove that I was upholding standards. Dr. Pat gave me a kiss. The anesthesiologist went to work and I was drugged into the easiest, fastest, deepest, darkest, quietest sleep I had ever experienced, a sleep so profound, so effortless, that to this day I wish I could do it again. And, come to think of it, one day I suppose I will. It was a sleep like death.

I lay in bed after the surgery, feeling as though I had been battered. My belly was swollen with air; within a week I looked like I was six or seven months pregnant, and in fact, that was how I felt. It all came back to me, in body memory, and I began to behave as though I were carrying a precious parcel inside of me: turning from side to side, I tenderly settled my belly in place. It was perverse, actually, because what I was carrying was the absence of a part of me. I had been told to get out of bed frequently, and to walk around, but it was difficult to move. I had never felt so tired. And of course, all I could think about was the invisible cell, the one I was sure had escaped, the cell that was going to burrow into my guts somewhere else and slowly strangle the life out of me.

Now that I know what it is like to be bedridden, I have a much clearer picture of how I should have prepared. If there is a next time, I will position my bed with a view out a big, clean window, with a birdfeeder stuck in the ground, and a drinks trolley stacked with books and my binoculars by my side. As it was, I gazed into the cracks in my ceiling as though at the Sistine Chapel, and watched the busy labor of the tiny spiders that had colonized the dim recesses of the picture molding.

Stroller's kind, solicitous ways upon learning that I had cancer lasted about two weeks, until I got out of surgery, whereupon he panicked and disappeared. Once again, the world divides into two types of people: those who are by your side through thick and thicker, and those who only like thin. Hospitals do strange things to people, especially the people who don't have to be in them. Illness brings out everyone's fears of being left behind, or being contaminated, or being inadequate to that challenge of making things right. I know; I've taken my turn being the one afraid to show up. Stroller was sullen in the hospital the day he came to sit with me. Only when I insisted did he relieve my tired sister. We would have fought about his bad attitude, but I was too groggy. I suppose he was going through some crisis of abandonment, but all I wanted to say was: *Sometimes it isn't about you.*

When he asked for the twentieth time, before the surgery, whether it was okay that he was going to London, I told him, Absolutely, please, I'm sure, no problem, go ahead and take that business trip. Who was I to be demanding? I absolutely did not want to cause anyone any inconvenience. I could take care of myself, right? Then he decided to leave a few days earlier, to get some shopping done.

So of course it was my fault he wasn't there to take me home from the hospital.

What did I know? I had never had cancer before.

My sister took me home, and my friend Caroline flew down from Boston carrying a box of her special chocolate chip cookies and a small crystal bell that I was to ring whenever I wanted her help.

Stroller phoned from London several times, cheer in his voice. He told me funny stories and was upbeat and charming. He put the concierge of the hotel on the phone to wish me well, and then called back with the salesman at the cheese shop, who told me to get better. He called on his way to the store to buy himself the colorful striped socks I found so endearing. But it hurt to laugh. I don't think he understood how difficult, how painful, it was to reach for the phone, how nearly impossible it was to hear about a trip that we were supposed to have been taking together. I don't think I understood how deeply I would come to resent his behavior at the hospital. I had wanted him to know that I needed him—without having to ask him to be there. I stopped answering the phone.

A few days later the biopsy was returned: not one, but two different kinds of tumors were smack in the middle of the kidney, one tucked slyly behind the other so that it hadn't even shown up on any of the screens. Both malignant.

Kidney cancer is referred to as a "silent killer." It is extremely slow-growing, but deadly. Nothing can cure it. It is one of the few cancers for which there is still no known chemotherapy. Radiation is useless. It is so dangerous that tumors deep in the kidney suspected of being cancerous are not even biopsied pre-surgery. The risk of a cell escaping during the extraction is too high. Most people—and they are generally older than I was, and generally male—do not know they have kidney cancer until they are peeing blood and otherwise symptomatic. By this time, it is often too late. In my case, the margins around the cancerous tissue in my kidney were clean, as the surgeon explained it. The cancer hadn't broken out of its host, and it likely had not spread. There was no statistical likelihood of the same thing occurring in the other kidney.

Kidney cancer has nothing whatsoever to do with kidney stones. Dr. Pat was highly intuitive. And careful. She had heard that I had had kidney trouble at an unusually young age, and thought, Let's just take a look. She saved my life.

And I was lucky. In fact, over the next year, I would lapse into dazes, wondering, *What if I hadn't decided to see a new doctor?*

What if I hadn't kept the appointment for the ultrasound? From time to time, I would wonder, *How far would the tumors have metastasized if they were still in me? When would I have started feeling ill? How much weight would I have lost? When would I have started dying?*— that sort of dark fantasy.

I had cheated death. For a week or two, I was full of gratitude and awe at the beauty of life's simplest pleasures. And then I started fleeing as fast as I could from the stark evidence of mortality. Against doctors' orders, I returned to work within weeks, way too early. Never mind that I couldn't even get through the day without lying down every couple of hours. I probably added months to my recovery by running myself ragged. At least I could feel needed. Dr. Pat, knowing something about the culture of Condé Nast, warned me not to tell anyone that I had had cancer. I took her advice. Weeks later, I was called into an executive's office to be questioned about my use of a car service, which had suddenly spiked. (I normally took a train to work.)

"I'm sorry, but I had no choice," I said. "I've had major surgery. For cancer. I'm still feeling weak."

"How long is this going to go on?" he said.

What kind of company is this? I thought, and then pushed it away. Was this worth it? Of course not. I should have taken better care of myself.

Several months after the surgery, Stroller announced, out of the blue, that he was not filing for that divorce after all. He had hired a lawyer and gone before a judge to redefend the status of his legal separation. He had won his case. But he would go no further. He was right back where he had started: legally separated, only with greater emphasis this time around. So it wasn't about his wanting to stay married, though, curiously, separation seemed to make marriage possible. There was something more profoundly wrong.

After the operation, I didn't want to stop and think too much. Reconsidering it all now, from the vantage of long days of unemployment, it strikes me how divorce became a mere symbol of the many ways in which Stroller kept me outside the ring of his life. Over the years, our postures of ambivalence, at once protective and depleting, had ossified, leaving me hungry for more. Something about having had a life-threatening illness had begun, slowly and quietly, to realign my tolerances—at a molecular level. My connection to Stroller had begun to thin; with the scene in the hospital, my heart lost its rebound. Sure, spontaneous and charming gestures were fun, but what about plain, old, everyday reliability? Didn't I care about that?

I was startled to realize that I had been using my fight with Stroller to avoid all the fights I should have been having with myself. I had been so angry with him—he made it so easy to be—that I didn't have to think about how angry I was with myself. It was always about him. What about my own craziness? I suddenly realized I didn't care any longer why *he* was wedded to ambivalence. Why was *I* so mired in it? Was I afraid to be alone? Was I afraid to let go of the suffering we shared? It was obvious, but there it was. Suddenly I realized that I couldn't change him. I could only change myself.

It just didn't seem necessary, or worth it, to return to the same frustrating dynamic, which was only about my wanting something I couldn't have, and him not wanting something he could have. Life, finally, was feeling too precious to waste time crying over self-inflicted sorrow. There was quite enough to be sad about that wasn't in my control. I can't say that this came as a blinding realization. I felt as though, during the surgery, I had burned through a lifetime, but it took nearly a year of falling apart, and of quiet, thoughtful solitude and self-examination, away from the intensely busy, deadline-driven world of the office, for me to finally claim cancer's gift: clarity.

Stroller and I never recovered, and I had to face it: we never would. Eventually, though, *I* did.

So you can see why Dr. Pat can check on the state of my underwear, the state of the scales, the state of my love life, the state of my ovaries, and the state of anything else she wants to, anytime she wants to. However, in the years following the operation, it has become clear that losing a kidney has done nothing to dampen my appetite. Losing a job didn't help matters, either. Thus, we can get back to the story of my morning visit to Dr. Pat for my checkup.

She puts me on the scales. Her eyes widen.

When Dr. Pat asks me how I am doing, I burst into tears.

By now you probably get the idea that there is no straight line out of depression, no light at the end of the tunnel, no tunnel, even. My operative image for my emotional state is that I am frequently in the woods. Sometimes I'm in the really dark parts, and it is damp and cold and I'm fearful and miserable, but sometimes

I wander into dappled light, which seems miraculously uplifting. (My idea of bliss is a sunny glade.) In the year after losing my job, I was doing a lot of wandering in the woods. When I go to see Dr. Pat, it so happens that I am backsliding into a dark patch.

My new weight isn't only about the joy of cooking muffins. Even I know that. I begin babbling my way through the litany. I have lost my job; I have finally given up on Stroller; my younger son has left home to go to college, so I'm truly living alone; I have been forced to put my house on the market, and the stock market has taken a nosedive, dragging along with it much of my life savings. Then, of course, there's also the fact that every cancer survivor worries about *the cell*. What if one miserable, minuscule cancer cell is going haywire in my body? What if that twinge I felt when I reached into the back of the pantry for the peanut butter wasn't a pulled muscle, but lung cancer? What if that throbbing pain wasn't a headache, but a brain tumor?

"It is all too much. I just feel I can't make anything right. I couldn't save my magazine. I couldn't save my relationship. I can't control anything. And global warming! I can't stop thinking about it. Have we discussed global warming yet? We are destroying our world. Do you realize this? And I've contributed to it. A lot! Everything has gone wrong and it is just too much."

By now I am sobbing. I am expecting to hear about a psychiatrist she wants me to see, or medication I could take to make it all better. I am prepared to tell her not to bother with that, that I had a terrific doctor but if he heard Stroller's name one more time I was sure he would fire me, too.

Dr. Pat sits quietly, looking at me, for a few moments.

"You've gained fifteen pounds," she says. "Time for you to go on Dr. Pat's Diet."

She reaches into a bag behind her desk, pulls out an impossibly cute, tiny can of V8 juice, wipes off the top, pops the tab, and hands it to me. "Drink this." She begins scribbling furiously on her notepad.

"The key is protein. And the trick is the V8 juice. You will eat very small portions. But you will eat throughout the day. No more meals. No more dinner parties. No more benefits. I don't care who's inviting you. You don't want to go to those anyway. Why would you? They're all boring. Stay home. Stay on the diet. E-mail me every night. Tell me what you ate.

"And this is important: Tell me about the saboteurs. What makes you break the regimen? Every night, I want an e-mail. And every morning, weigh yourself. And send me the number. Accurately."

I hold up my hand to ask a question.

"Yes, the V8 is salty. You need the salt. You need it for energy. You'll need to be able to keep going."

This is sounding ominous. I raise my hand again, but she cuts me off.

"The thing about this diet is that it will make you aware. It will make you aware of what you are eating. It will make you aware of when you are eating. Instead of all that mindless shoving of stuff into your mouth, you will learn to pay attention when you are full. You will understand why you are eating. And you'll think about how alcohol and sugar become a way of life. You don't want that way of life, I can assure you.

"And another thing. You have to get more exercise. It isn't too late. Yet. We need to reshape you. You work out. You stay on this diet for two months. You won't be able to do it longer. But I promise you, you will feel like a new person.

"One last thing. No wine. None. Whatsoever. It's all sugar. It goes right to your belly."

She makes puffing motions with her hands over her size 0 Marc Jacobs-clad stomach.

"Forget what you read in the papers. It isn't good for you. Not even one glass of wine. It isn't worth it."

I inquire timidly about liquor straight up, the kind that comes in screw-top bottles. My friend Jack Daniels? Laphroaig? She rocks back in her chair, waving her hands around the place where her belly would be if she had one.

"None. Whatsoever. All sugar. Your stomach."

I am, quite frankly, appalled. Never mind her demented attitude about alcohol. Here I am, brokenhearted, ready to spill out my grief in intimate detail, and there she is, handing me a suspiciously skimpy-looking page of scribbled detail about a diet.

I cannot begin to tell you the ways in which this entire enterprise is doomed, and the ways in which it offends me. When I leave Dr. Pat's office, the first problem that occurs to me, naturally enough, is of the implications for décor. I do not own a scale. It is a cliché of modern life that all single women own scales and keep them in the bathroom. Am I going to join that gang? A quick scan through several housewares stores convinces me that I would never own a scale. They are hideous. Why has no one designed a decent-looking modern scale? What is with the batteries, the large digital readouts, and the weird sliver shapes? What has happened to scales with heft and seriousness of purpose? Where have the dials gone, with their gorgeous serriffed numerals, and the beautifully crafted, delicate needles that shivered toward a number? What has happened to scales that let you jiggle the calibrations to help things along?

Of course, days later, when I finally do buy the sort of old-fashioned doctor's office scale I want—made in Germany, wouldn't you know it—I can't read the numbers from as far away as my head, and crouching down to see better causes other problems, like tipping over. Well, all I need is a rough guess.

Furthermore, I am certainly not going to get into the confessional spirit, e-mailing Dr. Pat every night, as I am not about to buy into the massive Food = Guilt psychosis of the developed world. I may not like to cook much, but I love it when other people cook for me. And as should be very clear by now: I love to eat. And drink.

After I settle the scale in my closet, I take the diet to the supermarket and stock up on the permissible food items—all four of them. It is then that I begin to feel the effects of the diet.

Massive relief.

No more gnawing insecurity about my food choices. No more chiding myself for my unimaginative ingredients. No more worrying about variety, or nutrition. No more decisions about food relatedness, recipes, balances, or any of it. No more even—or especially—worrying about local and organic. Liquid vegetables in cans have no roots. I type up Dr. Pat's notes, which turn into a sort of haiku that fills only three inches of paper—a pretty good visual representation of the contents. Even Dr. Pat's diets are size 0. I put copies in my pantry, in the refrigerator, in my datebook, in my handbag, anywhere that it might reach out and comfort me.

Wake	6 oz water, while still in bed
7:30	tea; boiled egg; bottle water
9:30	V8
11:30	fat-free cottage cheese (small container); $\frac{1}{2}$ apple; $\frac{1}{4}$ teaspoon cinnamon; 1 tablespoon ground flax seed; water
1:30	smallest water-packed tuna, or $\frac{1}{2}$ grilled skinless chicken breast; greens; bottle water
3:30	V8
5:30	fat-free cottage cheese, cinnamon, flax, $\frac{1}{2}$ apple
7:00	4 oz protein; 1 cup veggies (only broccoli, asparagus, zucchini, summer squash, green beans, cucumber); water
9:30	2 oz protein, preferably turkey; water

Any time of day, V8 juice, as much as desired

As I dutifully broil the week's supply of boneless, skinless, tasteless chicken breasts, I notice how simple it is to cook when your only worry is how to contain the flames shooting out of the heating element. It doesn't matter how the chicken is prepared. It isn't supposed to taste like anything. I begin to eat my salad like a rabbit, straight out of the bag. Things move along like clockwork: I have a schedule for what to eat and drink on awakening (when to wake up, no small accomplishment there). There is nothing to think about. And I am always eating.

This is by far the healthiest regimen I have ever maintained.

My e-mails to Dr. Pat involve matters of clarification: Exactly how much is 6 oz. of meat? "The size of a deck of cards." Exactly why can't I have Brussels sprouts? "Too many carbs." I am supposed to be telling her about when I trip up, and who or what situation undermined me. The saboteurs. Well, that is easy, but what is the point of telling her about dinner with my parents— "What's wrong with you? Why aren't you eating?" Dinner with anyone, for that matter. Dinner on an airplane. Dinner during job interviews. Dinner on dates. All impossible. What trips me up? Life. I have never considered how much of my life revolves around food.

And yet, dining has never been simpler. Cooking has never been easier. And those dumbbells! Yoga! I am unfurling limbs that have not been stretched in years. I am even learning, appropriately enough, to stand on my head. I smile at myself in the mirror and decide that a smile is the best sort of face-lift. I start smiling at everyone. Life has never been more peaceful. Within weeks, I am no longer obsessed with my problems. I am happily handing things over to other powers faster than the powers can present themselves. My mind is so warped that I understand with the force of revelation that I cannot control anything at all in the world except what I am eating. I cannot think about anything at all except my next supply of protein.

Within a month, I feel relieved of the burdens of the world. And fifteen pounds as well. I am now convinced that Dr. Pat is right about everything. Even her attitude about the alcohol isn't so crazy.

All I know is that, once again, I have the illusion that my life is in order. And sometimes that's as good as it gets.

By summer I am an old pro at sleeplessness. I have learned not to stay in bed at five in the morning. What's the point? I make a strong cup of tea with hot milk, and step out into the dewy gray light to inspect yesterday's planting. I look to see if everything has made it through the night. As I tossed and turned, I worried that I might have buried the iris too deep, or been too rough dividing the hosta. I've been fretting over my plants as if they were newborns, as fearful that I might nip off a bud as a new mother taking scissors to her infant's silky fingernails.

A light rain begins to fall. A couple of sparrows flutter up toward the corners of my house's tall sheets of windows, and I see that they are nipping at spiders and their neatly wrapped prey—no wonder those corners have stayed clean. I'm full of admiration for the way the natural world not only adjusts to our presence, but also takes advantage of it. Here's this new house, plunked down in the middle of a meadow. But look again, here's this new way to trap insects.

I've logged ten-hour days in this garden over the last few weeks. I realize that it may be a futile effort, given the salt air, the wind, and the deer, but I can't help myself. I cannot have a home without a garden. Mint is not enough. I've decided to be serious about resurrecting life from the dirt that surrounds this new building.

Gardeners will always make gardens; we can't help ourselves. And when we don't, we are no longer gardeners. End of story. It is a state of being. People who garden are their own peculiar tribe, compelled to get their hands into the earth. I recognize my behavior as a form of adaptation to habitat. Gardening has been the way I've made myself feel at home every place I've lived as an adult. Some people settle in by decorating; some get to know the neighbors; some explore the shops. Gardeners have to dig, and leave their trace on a patch of earth. Gardens teach you one lesson quickly: There is no such thing as a Forever Garden. Be brave. Nurture fortitude. It is only in the act of creating, in the endless planting and feeding and watering, in the living and dying and living again that forever might be found.

Every day, for weeks, all I want to do is dig holes, mix together a thick batter of compost and soil, and move plants around to see what looks good from this window or that door.

All I want to know in life now is the answer to the question: *Where does everything go?* Not in the sense of ultimate destination: Where do souls go when bodies decompose? Where does love go when it dies? Or even, as my children once asked, where does the sun go at the end of the day? Those sorts of questions once preoccupied me. No longer. Now what I want to know is, where does everything go? As in, where does this belong?

Where should these azaleas be planted? Where should I place the hellebores? For that matter, what drawer, in this new household, holds the knives? And which cupboard the screw-drivers? Where am I putting my pencils? Which closet is for brooms? Where do I put old diaries, old letters, old drafts?

Some patterns are so deeply ingrained as body memories that I will always look for the matches in the shallow drawer next to the sink, no matter where the sink is or what house it belongs to, no matter that there is no shallow drawer next to the sink. I reach first, think next. This is what makes discordant music so interesting to play: the mind reaches for a note in a known scale before understanding that the key has been breached, ruptured, or altogether ignored. However, playing piano is not the same as keeping house, and it is not interesting to be constantly looking for the dustpan. Rather, it is important to know where to find it, always, thoughtlessly, so as not to waste time on frivolous matters. And, come to think of it, this is why it is so very irritating to reach a time in life when you need not just one but two or three or even four pairs of glasses. How to know where to put one set of glasses when you reach for another? The time wasted looking for glasses could be spent rereading Tolstoy. Where do glasses go, in some sort of designated control-center bowl, waiting to be retrieved in the event of a near or far sighting?

The irritation of losing glasses, however, pales by comparison to the panic that fills your throat when you lose your cell phone, especially if you have forsaken the landline and that slim, slippery sliver of technology has become your only connection to the world. I learned never to take mine into the garden the day it slid from my pocket into a hole I'd begun to fill, and it took me a long, zany moment to understand the muffled music coming up out of that shallow grave. What's truly mindless, though, is to be frantically searching for your cell phone while you are in the middle of a long and complicated discussion with your best friend . . . on your cell phone.

Planting has its choreography: the stooping, the scraping, the mounding, the tamping. When I can no longer maintain the tempo of digging, I switch to weeding, and when that, too, winds down, my forearm cramped, I switch to pruning. Each movement is satisfying; each is exhausting. Gardening has its motifs, too, and its digressions. Within a week of buying plants and finding out where they belong, positioning them among the few trees and shrubs already there, I realize that I am re-creating the woodland garden I made at my old house, which itself was a re-creation of the garden my father made when I was a child— my first garden, imprinted forever within me as the way a garden ought to look.

At first, I think I must still be depressed, even though I thought I was doing better. Why else would I be spending hour upon hour doing something as inane as digging holes? Why else would I think that I should turn a meadow into a forest? But then, at some point, usually accompanied by the sound of the clanging shovel or the sharp odor of the compost, I realize how happy I am, and how lucky. I'm unafraid. I'm taking care of myself. As Mary Oliver writes, "You too can be carved anew by the details of your devotions."

If I wanted to, I could grow my own dinner.

I don't want to, though.

What's more, I notice I'm becoming something of a min-iaturist. Suddenly, a bare stone path offends my aesthetic sen-sibility. I never used to bother with such places, never saw the appeal of tiny, creeping plants. Perhaps the glasses are helping. Alpine plantings, with their half-carat flowers, never caught my eye. But this garden is small, so I'm taking advantage of every inch. Suddenly, the tourmaline chip of a dianthus, or the seed pearl of the thumb-sized sedum, is very appealing. I'm digging dozens of fist-sized holes, squeezing thyme and saxifrage into cracks.

I have no idea what will make it, how much sun anything will really get, what the drainage is like (though I can see where the puddles take a while to seep into the soil, if you can call this compacted post-construction gray matter soil; it looks more like the mixings for cement, and feels that way, as my shovel rings against it, the vibrations racing up my arm and down into my already troubled back). Over the years, though, I've learned not to worry so much about what will or won't make it: I'm learning the "So what?" lesson. So what if it fails? That doesn't mean it was all a mistake. So what if it ends? That doesn't mean it should never have begun. I've seen, too, how things thrive in the most unlikely places. Sun-loving plants sometimes estab-lish themselves in deep shade. They just take on the attenuated, melancholic inclination of those creatures of the gloaming.

A couple of bedraggled blueberry bushes have miracu-lously made it through the construction, looking only a little worse for the wear. I'm grateful, because they were a gift from my father, who has lately begun to brood about dying, or, as he puts it with a little too much cheer, "corking off." He tells me he isn't afraid of it; I guess he has seen so much of death in his life as a surgeon. But I wonder how ready he is; his health is perfect, but many of his friends have passed away. I wonder, too, whether the blueberry bushes were part of his preparation. As I transplant them to a nicer spot in the sun, I remember the day we first put them in. I will always think of them as the Don't Tell Your Mother blueberries.

"Here. Let's put them here," he was saying, as we walked to the shed for a shovel. "Right here, near the privet; there's plenty of sun. You won't let the mower run over them, will you?"

My shovel was rusted and dirty; I hadn't cleaned my tools before putting them away for the winter. It was the wrong sort of tool for the job he had in mind, and he, having had the correct tools placed in his open palm at the precise moment he needed them throughout his entire working life as a surgeon, would be sure to complain.

"This isn't the sort of shovel I need. The bottom is flat. The ground is too hard. Haven't you got a spade with a rounded edge? I'm getting too old for this sort of work. Too old. Too tired. Get me another shovel."

"That's it, Daddy. That's the only shovel I have. The ground is hard because this is the lawn, Daddy. You are about to dig holes in my lawn."

"Lawn?" he snorted. "You can hardly call this a lawn. We are digging a new bed, chickpea. This gift needs a new bed. Don't tell your mother. She won't like it. She says I spoil you."

He began to dig.

By the time of this gift, my father was into his old age and frequently querulous; he was constantly talking about how we would have to shoot him when he became too addled to take care of himself, which was sure to happen any day now. He could feel the end of his life, he said. I could not imagine the world without him in it. I was already accustomed to his casual references to death.

When we were small children, he would set up the old slide projector on the table after dinner, and prop a screen up on an easel across the room. Lined up on our little wooden chairs, our hair washed and brushed and braided, our pajamas freshly ironed, his three daughters would watch spellbound as he reviewed pictures of the operations he would be doing. I would sit closest to him, my chair pulled up close to the screen because I was so nearsighted, being careful not to utter a shriek or groan of disgust. I would feel that I was inside the great, shining, throbbing, purple aneurysm as my father described the procedure for removing it, what could go wrong. He was meticulous in his explanations, and grateful for the audience.

"Don't tell your mother what I've been showing you. She finds it revolting. You're the only ones who understand my work," I remembered he always said to us.

We had driven to a nursery many miles away because he had suddenly, while visiting me, decided that it was imperative that I have blueberry bushes in my garden. The trip took longer than we had planned and he was fretful about what he would tell my mother when we got back—why had we been away so long, what had we been doing? But when we got to the nursery he was happy, and, as he chatted up a friendly flirtation with the robust saleswoman who drove a golf cart, we toured the grounds. Before we got to the blueberry section, he piled into the wagon gallons of hostas, clematis, daylilies, foxgloves. Full sun to full shade, it made no difference. Everything was appealing. The foxgloves were especially admirable. Digitalis. I wished I could slip my own little paw into the pendulous, velvety apricot gloves, wished I could breathe into my lungs the narcotic that would regulate my heart. When we finally got home again, I barely had the energy to plant everything. But my father was fine, ready to get to work.

"This is a good place for the blueberries. You'll always think of me when you look at them," he was saying, digging quickly and efficiently, hardly out of breath.

He tapped three straggling blueberry bushes out of their plastic containers.

"Trowel, please," he said, his back to me, his hand out, palm up. Just like in the operating room. I got to be the nurse.

He tamped the soil firmly around the railed stems. The bushes didn't look as if they could produce more than seven berries among them.

"You'll make blueberry pies for the children, you'll make blueberry cobblers, you'll make blueberry ice cream, you'll eat blueberries with your cereal and milk, and you'll think of me.

"Hose, please."

I placed it in his palm.

The water gushed and pooled around the plants.

"One day you'll remember how we went to the nursery, and bought these plants, and came back to your house and planted them together. I'll be gone, and years from now you will have more blueberries than you can eat. You will look at the blueberries and you will think of me. You will water them, won't you? You won't let them dry up? You won't let them die?"

No, Daddy, I won't let them die. Sometimes I feel like I am the fulcrum of a seesaw on which my children are going up in their lives, and my parents are coming down. It is all I can do to maintain equilibrium. I dig and dig, and dig some more. I've taken to wearing my children's castoffs in the garden and, I admit it, around town from time to time, too. My baggy skateboard pants are now covered with dirt, the knees encased in mud. Dirt is smeared across my face, where my fingers have pushed back my hair and my glasses, and all over my shirt. It gives me profound pleasure to be so dirty.

A tiny bee climbs down my neck; I'm unaware of it until I feel a prick on my shoulder. Shaking out my shirt, I feel another prick on my back, and then, as the bee frantically escapes into my pants, a weak pinch on my leg, then all is quiet. I find the tiny, crumpled body nestled in the top of my sock.

I stop and lean on my spade to watch worms, suddenly finding themselves exposed to light, wriggle their way back into the soil, how their pointed mouths burrow into the earth, how their bodies expand and contract, how small but significant lumps seem to get pushed down their rosy lengths. Worms, like tortoises, like children, seem to take forever to get anywhere, but turn your attention away and they are gone by the time you think to look again. It is a challenge to watch a worm long enough for it to bury itself completely—a perennial piece of theater, but until now I've never made it past the first act.

By the end of the day, I'm sitting on the ground. It has taken me a while to achieve such intimacy with the earth. In the morning, I'm bending to reach the plants; by midday, I'm squatting; by mid-afternoon, I'm on my knees, careful not to land on the brittle, razor-edged holly leaves littering the ground. By late afternoon, I'm tired, my legs are cramping, and I'm happy to release myself to the gravity of the earth. Long minutes drift by as I sit on the ground. I've dropped like a rag doll, unable to move. A couple of finches peck at the mulch by my feet. A dove walks past at a stately pace. A hummingbird scissors the air above my head. I found one on the terrace not long ago, a bird so small that I could shroud its broken body in an ivy leaf fastened with a pine needle. This one zips down and waggles her tail in my face. Perhaps I am sitting too near her babies. I'm sorry, I can't move. Instead, in her honor, I review what I know about hummingbirds: tongues thin as thread; feet poor for walking; eggs the size of peas; nests the size of walnuts, made of dandelion fluff and spider silk. I may have made that last bit up, embroidering with the silk. I want it to be true. Sometimes it is hard to leave off desiring for reality.

Dusk falls. The peepers come out, their rhythmic, rattling exhalations the lullaby of summer evenings. I let my gaze wander over the topsoil, spotting the tiny spiderwebs spun from leaf to leaf, glistening in the low sunlight; the cricket resting on a stone. I begin to appreciate the Jains of India, who sweep the ground ahead of them as they walk so as not to destroy a living soul in their path. There is so much in our paths that we never notice; we wreak untold havoc crossing a field. But . . . so what? I will never have the patience, the delicacy, or the terrible goodness—I'll never even have the desire—to sweep all life out from under each molesting step. So I push the Jain bead to an ever-growing column on my moral abacus, the column marked "life's too short." For all of us.

While I'm on the ground, I make a mental inventory of the patches of weeds that threaten to choke off the lilies, the rampant clematis already laced through the lilac, the tendril of bittersweet getting a toehold near the wall. That bittersweet is a clever pest; just as a feverish person can seem, at first glance, to be blushing with good health, a plant smothered in new bitter will look lush and fresh.

And still I sit. There is always tomorrow for what can't get done today. Making lists of tomorrow's chores must be a way of shoring up against that childhood anxiety—"What is there to do? There is nothing to do." All children say this, repeatedly, whiningly, annoyingly. I said it often as a child, my inner resources not yet grown in. I remember my father telling me, with mocking exasperation, to go twiddle my thumbs. So I did, for several hours, just to prove that I was desperate to be given something to do, and I would do anything, no matter how boring—that's how utterly, devastatingly bored I was with nothing to do.

Today I am happy to find myself sitting on the ground wanting nothing to do—no, not even wanting it, simply accepting that I am enveloped in nothing to do. I begin to understand how nothing to do is its own state of grace, difficult to find deliberately, nearly impossible to recognize. Nothing to do means I can sit and look and let my mind wander, then empty, then fill again, with wonder or with grief, with anything or with nothing at all. "Nothing to do" is not the same as "Nothing can be done." One is hopeless; the other, the place from which hope becomes possible.

18 . THE BEST SUMMER EVER

PERVERSELY LATE IN the game, I have been cast unwittingly into the role of a stay-at-home mom. I keep thinking there is poetic justice at work, retribution from the angry god who lives in a tiny crack in my brain, and who believes mothers should never leave their children, ever.

"I am a stay-at-home mom," I tell myself, rehearsing in case I'm asked what I am doing with myself these days. It is true. I am spending most of my time at home. And I am a mom. The problem is that I am not with my children, as they are no longer living anywhere near home, which in any case is no longer *ours*. I am struck by the lopsidedness of this situation. "I am a stay-at-home mom but my children are no longer at home," I repeat endlessly. I even write it down. First it comes out looking like an invitation or an announcement of some sort:

I am a
Stay-at-Home Mom
But
My Children
Are No Longer
At Home

RSVP, please!

Then I try writing it out in free verse, hoping that I might capture the essence of a madness stealing over my heart:

I am a stay-at-home Mom
But my children
Are no longer home.

The more I think about it, the more unnerving it becomes, until finally I am hallucinating conversations with that relentlessly angry god nattering away in my brain.

ANGRY GOD: So, you wanted a career?

PATHETIC MOM: Yes, but I wanted my children, too.
                I wanted it all.

ANGRY GOD: So. See what happens? You got nothing.

PATHETIC MOM: But that's not true! I got a lot! I went to
                open school nights. I went to PTA meet-
                ings. I went to plays and I walked my
                boys to school. And then I went to sales
                meetings! I sat in boardrooms! I read
                spreadsheets!

ANGRY GOD: How many hours did you spend at
                work? How many hours did you spend
                at home? You do the math, Pathetic
                Mom.

PATHETIC MOM: But we had dinner together every night
                they were with me.

ANGRY GOD: In a restaurant? You call that dinner?
                          You didn't even cook every night. Look
                          at you now. No kids. No career.

I keep working it over. It had seemed worth the constant juggling of time and train schedules to create something that others might enjoy. But how many times had I missed a train? Gotten home late for dinner? Been too tired to spend enough time helping a child with his homework? The classic guilt syndrome of the working mother. Or of any working parent—but it is dawning on me that I still somehow thought women were supposed to have had a choice about going to work. Well, they did have a choice, if they played the marriage card correctly. It crosses my mind, with a bitter sting, that Stroller's wife had it made. Her salary as an ex dwarfed mine, and it was one hundred percent reliable. In fact, having been fired is what guaranteed it.

One morning Theo calls from college to announce that he is going to live in the new house in Rhode Island for the summer. Note that he does not say he is going to live *with me* in the new house in Rhode Island. He fully expects that I will be back at work by then and that he, also at work at a local beach club, will have the house to himself. He plans to get a lot done: surfing, meditating, writing, and recording music.

He is, therefore, a bit nonplussed on his arrival when, after helping him unpack, do his laundry, make his bed, and cook him dinner, I do not get into my car and hit the road. Nor do

I leave the following week. In fact, I am on quite a good writing streak; I have assignments to complete. My consulting jobs have wound down, and I see no reason to go anywhere.

"Don't you want to visit those friends you're always talking about, Mom?" he asks a few times. "The ones in Maine?" By now he wouldn't mind if I were planning to live in Antarctica.

Well, I do go to Maine, and I drive through upstate New York, too, but only for a few days, as I always miss my own bed. What's more, I am having a splendid time finally being Theo's stay-at-home mom. I get him up and make him tea every morning. I feed him muffins fresh from the oven, as I am back to baking at the crack of dawn, filling the house with wonderful smells. I drive him to the beach for work when it is too rainy for a bicycle ride. I greet him at the door in the evening, and we sit down for a home-cooked dinner every night. Theo even takes a few turns in the kitchen, and he is more freewheeling with the recipes than I am, concocting a few surreal and delicious pasta sauces that do double duty in cleaning out the fridge.

Once I tell my friends that I am cooking for Theo every night, and entertaining the idea of moving to a new level of expertise, they send me more recipes, cheering me on. Even so, I secretly want to go straight to making desserts. My holy grail is Caroline's Chocolate Chip Cookies, or more accurately, her mom's. Caroline is a hearty, enthusiastic cook, who once invited all her friends to submit their favorite fast recipes for a weeknight cookbook she was compiling. I'm mortified to confess that I sent in a recipe for The Suburban Mom's Whiskey Sour, which involved shortcuts with frozen lemonade for all those times when you need a drink but haven't any fresh fruit in the fridge. Someone has to be realistic.

Mom's Chocolate Chips Cookies are a variation on the Nestlé Toll House theme, but that's like saying the *Goldberg Variations* are a simple matter of remixed notes. Caroline doesn't keep secret recipes, but not a single one of her friends has been able to replicate her cookies, which are thin, delicate discs with a perfect snap, whose golden dough serves only to hold the dark, melting chips in a crackle of lace. I have been trying for years to make them, but the proportions never work, perhaps because I always add more chips.

Theo comes in one afternoon and grabs a handful of gooey experimentation.

"Mom, this is just like my music," he says, devouring a fistful of cookies. "I lay down a track of synthesizer that I really like, and if there's a nice sound I might amp it up even more in the mix, but then it overpowers everything and no one can catch the subtle intricacies of the music. These aren't cookies. They're chocolate." But he eats them anyway.

"Are you sure there isn't a typo in the recipe?" I ask Caroline one hot midsummer morning. "Do you think it's the humidity here? They're all limp. Are you sure you didn't skip something when you were writing this up?"

"I know, I know," she says. "Everyone is complaining about this recipe. Everyone is accusing me of holding something back. I'm not. I'm sharing. I swear. It's just tricky."

For the twentieth time, I review the steps.

"You've got it all right," she says.

"Then why am I unable to make your cookies?"

That's when it hits me. Those cookies have nothing to do with flour or eggs or water. They are about her touch, her spirit. Cooking has nothing to do with ingredients, and everything to do with love—that's why anyone with the desire can cook. All those years, thinking I couldn't cook, I could have been cooking my heart out.

"I have an idea," says Caroline, interrupting my thoughts. "You need me to come down and show you how to make them."

And she did.

I am having the happiest summer of my adult life. I, who was once afraid to throw a dinner party, love having people at my table—and having the time and the energy to deepen old friendships and develop new ones. I love spending hours with my son, and enjoy the strange philosophical discussions we get into, about his interest in Buddha and the Tao, and his desire to let go of materialism, to live more simply (after the summer is over, of course) and to become more mindful of waste. All of this touches me, and reminds me of what it was like to have a nineteen-year-old brain.

Until, one evening, Theo asks me when I am leaving.

"Leaving?" I said.

"Yeah. You know, like, going back to New York to get a job."

"Why on earth would I do that, Theo? I love being here with you. In fact I've just been thinking how this is the best summer I have ever had. And I have enough work to do right here. I have assignments. I have deadlines to meet. I'm finally writing again. It's weird. As soon as I got the boxes unpacked, and the garden going, I was able to type. I thought it was all over for me as a writer. Maybe it's like a Zen kind of thing, you know, as though I needed to be grounded, in a literal sort of way . . ."

I trail off. Theo is focused on a vague middle distance behind my head. He doesn't seem too interested in my existential dilemma. He is having one of his own.

"Well, you know, I kind of thought I would have a summer of solitude, you know, a summer where I just lived on my own, you know, like, making money and supporting myself."

I look around at the new house, the new garden, the view out over the pond, the Atlantic surf pounding beyond. A wave of fury breaks over my head. I can no longer remember exactly what happens next, but I can assure you that it's something along the lines of my telling him that if *he* wants *me* to leave *my* house, he has another thing coming, and that if he wants to support himself without me around, there is the door, and he's welcome to go to an island somewhere far away and live in a room and wait tables and spend his own money on rent and food.

Fine, says Theo, and picking up a gallon of water, he slams out of the house and bicycles away, no doubt heading for that island idyll.

I am dumbfounded. Here I am, having the best summer ever, and there he is, building up a head of steam about how he is spending his summer with his mom. And no, it isn't about a girl. I ask.

Have I raised a little Stroller, a man who wants to be with me, but doesn't want to be with me? Is this normal? Why am I feeling unwelcome in my own house?

All of a sudden I understand why this fight with my son is so difficult for me. I have not lived with anyone for longer than three or four days at a time *in fifteen years*. Not with my children, who had to shuttle between their father and me after our divorce—but come on, only a few blocks! Give me a break, Angry God! Not with the men I dated, who never got so far into my life as to move into my house. I have had intimacy, I have had love, I have had constancy, but I have not had anyone day in and day out.

And, what's worse, *I never even noticed*, until the fight with Theo.

A few hours later, Theo marches back into the house and apologizes.

"It's just weird, Mom, having you around all the time. I mean, it's like you're my wife or something."

I am beginning to believe it is my fate to become a living, breathing, walking, talking illustration of Freudian theory.

"You're there when I come home, and you ask me how my day was. That's what a wife does. I don't want you to be a stay-at-home mom."

I ask him if what this all means is that he is sorry that I didn't stay at home with him all day during his childhood.

"Yeah, right, Mom. I hate the way I turned out. And it's all your fault because you went to work. Get it? Come on!"

I do get it. He is a wonderful, growing person. He loves life. He has good values. He asks the important questions. He tries to be considerate of other people. And he knows he is loved by both his father and his mother. I tell him so every chance I get. It turns out, I learn, that he is angry and unnerved that I have lost my job; it makes him anxious about his own future. What's the point, he wants to know, of working so hard and for so long only to see your career smashed? I try to phrase my answer in a way that makes sense to him: the pleasure is in the doing—and suddenly I realize, amazingly, that finally I believe that, too. So what if it ends? The adventure was wonderful. There's more ahead.

With that conversation, the skies clear. The rest of the summer sails by and the days are filled with peace and contentment. Theo writes fifteen songs and records them, singing and playing a few different instruments. I feel even better than a stay-at-home mom. I feel like a child again, playing house: doing my work, sweeping the floor, baking cookies, reading books, pouring tea—doing anything I want to do, whenever I want to. I love being home; I love making a home.

I have to admit that after years of worrying about everything and everyone at work, years of managing people, years of deadlines and interrupted vacations, years of showing up and being strong, it is a pleasure to worry only about my small patch of ground. I love sitting quietly and writing.

Stroller doesn't even come into my thoughts very often anymore. When he does, I wonder why I broke my heart trying to make him happy, when he didn't even know if he wanted to be happy. Why did I spend so many years hanging around like a wide-mouth bass, just waiting to grab that baited hook for another fight? Why, at this time in my life, would I want to be around anyone who does not turn his face to joy and sunlight when there is a choice? Why did I have to become entangled in his problems? He did the best he could. And then again, so did I. We went as far as we could go. This summer marks the end of suffering over Stroller. As if the warmth of the season were working its magic, the pain simply melts away, and with it, the exhausting, irredeemable yearning.

Looking back on all the troubles with Stroller, I think I see what it was about. Just two people pushing against each other in fear. Suddenly the fight goes out of me. And in its place comes laughter. The things that once tormented me, his boyish temper, the way he shoved me out the door and then wanted me to come back, my frustrated wishes—those most of all; how much I wanted our lives intertwined in a constant, sturdy, reliable love, and how much I tried to battle my way to that, determined to carry him to that place even if he didn't want to be there—it all seems funny now. Comical and ludicrous.

I don't need Stroller to rescue me. I miss his wonderful ways, his charm, the things we shared. But I don't miss the drama. I don't miss the triangle. I don't miss being the object of someone's ferocious ambivalence. At the time, I found a heady romance in futility; I could keep dreaming about how wonderful things would be "someday." Hope glimmered for the future. I no longer want to live a life of expectation. If Stroller didn't grasp what I had to offer, it wasn't my fault. I was tired of clenching my fists around hope. Finally, I let it go. In return, I found peace. And gratitude.

All those inner resources that I have spent a lifetime developing have finally started kicking in again—those soul-saving habits of playfulness, most of all: reading, thinking, listening, being a friend, simply feeling my body move through the world, and finally, being open enough to notice the small beauty in every single day. The healing balm was there all along, nestled in a sofa that beckoned me to pick up a book, hovering outside the window inviting me to take a walk. It was just a matter of finding room in my life again for everything I love, and letting the quiet of solitary moments steal over my heart.

I remember something Stroller once said to me: "I no longer believe in the power of adult love to endure." We were in Paris, one of our favorite places to visit together. Stroller had become deeply interested in the life and work of the nineteenth-century painter Edouard Manet. We made pilgrimages to the Musée d'Orsay to see his works *Le déjeuner sur l'herbe* and *Olympia*. We went to the Musée Marmottan Monet, and lingered over the charming work of Berthe Morisot, who had been Manet's friend and, Stroller had become convinced, his true love. How else, but from a place of profound cherishment, could Manet have painted the stunning portrait of her we saw that morning? Manet and Morisot could not marry because Manet was already married—to a woman who had once been his piano teacher and may have been his father's mistress. Manet had married her when his father died, before he met Morisot. Morisot eventually married Manet's brother.

Stroller had been quite taken by the story of this tangled, triangulated ménage. As we wandered around, he imagined his way through the painter's frustrations, his despair, clearly identifying with Manet, seeing traces of lost love in his paintings. We decided to visit Manet's grave, and after taking many wrong turns through the 16th arrondissement on a dreary, wet day, we finally found the Cimetière de Passy. It took even longer to find Manet, because every time we asked the guards for help, they tried to send us to Père Lachaise cemetery. "Morrison? Jim Morrison? Of course. All Americans want to see Jim Morrison. Another place. Go. *Allez-y.*"

Finally, by accident, we wheeled around a corner and stumbled onto Manet's plot. We stood for a moment in silence, and then, in the same moment, we both gasped. We had suddenly noticed that there were three names engraved on the monument. Manet was joined in his grave by his wife— and by Berthe Morisot. All three—man, wife, and mistress— commemorated on one plot, united in death, their remains rotting away together.

Stroller was at first delighted with the audacity of such a situation, and then he grew pensive. We began, once again, to talk about the futility of coming to an agreement about how to proceed with our lives together. The evidence of Manet's solution, moldering in the bowels of the earth, left me cold.

"I no longer believe in the power of adult love to endure," Stroller said. "Things don't last. People make too many mistakes."

"You don't have a lifetime ahead of you anymore," I replied, rather meanly, I thought at the time. But now, remembering that moment, I am impressed by the inadvertent weight of a spontaneous truth.

"Don't worry, Stroller," I said, lifting my face to the cold drizzle. "If you're lucky, you have a good fifteen years left. Maybe twenty. Love doesn't have to endure so long anymore."

THE WIND OFTEN dies down in the afternoon. The pond is a glassy black; it is a good time to go out in the kayak. Theo has returned to school, the summer renters have left as well, and the whole town seems to breathe easier, decongested. I have been alone for the last week, enjoying an unusual amount of solitude—no visitors, no dinner parties, no deadlines, and no need for phone calls. Just my piano, my journal, my books, and the coyotes, foxes, minks, otters, raccoons, possums, bats, birds, snakes, and owls at my doorstep.

It will be an easy trip across the pond to the barrier beach, where I'll take a long walk and a swim in the ocean before dinner. I get the paddle and rubber boots out of the garage. It gives me pleasure to set out on this journey with a small bag containing only what will fit with me in the boat: goggles and a towel. My field glasses hang from my neck. I have a debate with myself about the cell phone. That old anxiety, but am I really going to need to call the coast guard for rescue? I don't want to become unable to disconnect. Trouble will wait. Good news ripens in delay. I set off without the phone.

I head out the back door and down the path mowed through the meadow to the edge of the water. I am careful not to step in a small creature's hole. If I wrenched an ankle, who would help me? I'm annoyed at that tinny voice that natters through my days. My parents, my sister, my children, and my friends all tell me to be careful. Don't swim by yourself. Don't go so far out. Don't use the kayak alone. Don't leave your doors unlocked. What are you doing up there, all by yourself? They're expressing love, I remind myself. But their worry is contagious, making me nervous, and I get the distinct feeling that they disapprove of my solitude; it also makes them anxious. So be it. I have finally come to embrace it. Someone once explained to me the difference between an introvert and an extrovert: both can enjoy going to a party, but the extrovert is energized by society, whereas the introvert has to recover from it. My batteries get drained easily these days, and need recharging in silence. Alone, I am willingly, cheerfully thrown upon myself.

It has been a beautiful September day, and the air is fresh and clear. What a gift to be able to go where I want. I am no longer young, but after all, I am not yet so old. Although I worry about pulled muscles, I am not at all frail. Even though I live alone, I live in the watchful care of loving friends and family. I take a deep breath, feel my lungs stretch against my ribs, and blow out the day's fears. I am strong, healthy, vibrant, and thankful. I have the energy and the will to get going. I have learned by now that getting going is the most important thing.

My little boat is a poky, squat, plastic affair, but it sits high—helpful in shallow water—and it is stable. It is dark green, to blend with the field in which I keep it, upside down, so it doesn't fill with rain. I flip it over. It does fill with ants and spiders and pill bugs, which I wipe out before dragging the boat down to the water. The thing may be ugly, but it fits me, or I fit it, and that is satisfying.

I ease one end of the boat into the pond, pushing through a gap in the cattails, which are so tall they hide me. Good thing, too, because the sight of me getting into the boat is comical, if not embarrassing. The water is so low I have to take a step into the muck to get the boat out far enough to float it. I've done this maneuver a hundred times, but I'm surprised by my awkwardness, my stiff knees. They actually creak. I have to move slowly, which means my foot is sucked deep into the mud before I wrench it out, give the boat a wobbly push, and crouch into the seat in the bottom. I'm fine once I'm settled. Feeling thankful again for their cover, I back out of the cattails.

I turn my boat around and get the hang of the paddle. The cormorants gathered on a rock have spread open the shiny black capes of their oily-feathered wings to dry. The swans drift away; there were at least a hundred on the pond this summer. "What'd you do?" a friend once asked. "Call Disney? This place is out of central casting." They are mute swans. They came here, the story goes, from Long Island, where a wealthy man had imported them to his estate from England in the '20s: the queen's own swans. I had seen the same kind on the Thames. When the man lost his fortune in the crash of '29, the grounds went to ruin, and the swans left to feed from other ponds. Their population no longer controlled, they spread across Long Island and then came north into Connecticut and Rhode Island. They are beautiful and nasty. They are fiercely territorial, and when threatened they attack—bodies high, necks thrusting, beaks wide and hissing, enormous wings flapping so powerfully they could easily snap my arm in two. It is not difficult to imagine how poor Leda was carried off by a swan to be raped. From time to time the swan population begins to overwhelm this marsh pond; the birds' necks are so long that they feed easily off the shallow bottom. They make it difficult for the smaller ducks to find nourishment. Some of the swans keep their necks underwater so long that their feathers become green with algae. Every once in a while someone starts a population control program, addling the large eggs and leaving them in the nests to fool the swans into slowing their production. It doesn't seem to work for long. Lately, though, some of the swans, perhaps feeling crowded, have pioneered the short flight to settle on Martha's Vineyard.

My arms ache, though I am not very far across the water. Taking the island that sits squarely in front of my house as a midway point, I give myself a rest. I balance my paddle across my lap, and as the boat drifts gently, I take an inventory of the other houses around the pond.

I've often wondered where home really is, for those of us (most of us) who don't live where we were raised or where we raised our children. I've finally decided that home is not necessarily where you live all the time; it is where you want to be when you die, where you want to be buried or have your ashes spread. Or perhaps it is the place where you feel most alive and true to yourself. This pond, then, is home to me, at least for now. I've come to accept that I can't count on anything to be permanent and it no longer matters. I know that if I ever leave this home, I will make another. If I ever lose my garden, I will plant another. What I crave is a place that slows me down and reconnects me with nature, the sea, the trees, the night cries of the animals. I picked this place to be my home; I wasn't born into it. I picked it, and now I have grown into it.

At rest in my kayak, I hear the commotion before I can find it—the loud pumping of wings. I raise my field glasses up as I twist around in my seat, in time to see the huge bird, its belly flushed with the late afternoon sun. It hangs, treading the air, suspended in place, wings beating fiercely, neck craned, head trained on the water, and then suddenly the osprey plunges, feetfirst, into the pond. When it comes up, it is holding a fish, its talons gripping the writhing creature over the top of its back so that the fish looks like it is flying horizontally through the air. The fish thrashes frantically from side to side, swimming still, as it was moments ago when it was plucked from its path. Its blue-gray and white scales catch the light, setting off a sparkle of sequins. The osprey, now skimming over the pond, squeezes its fingerlike claws. The strong, thick talons pierce deeper into the gills. Blood streams through the sky.

The osprey flies heavily toward the woods bordering the pond. No matter how many times I have seen this deathly spectacle, it horrifies and thrills me. I have been given the honor of witnessing a sacred ritual. I train my glasses on the osprey as it comes to rest on the uppermost limb of a tall, gnarled, and leafless tree at the edge of a meadow. With most of its rotting branches snapped off by storms, it has become a piece of sculpture, the suggestion of a tree. Its bark has been polished smooth and silvered by winds carrying fine sand. Its jagged form etches a lightning bolt against the greenish black of the leafy woods. The bird sits at the top, proudly, I can't help but think, though it is only its nature to hunt successfully. The bird gives a few short, shrill whistles and then hunches over its prey. The fish continues the frenzied folding of its long, taut body. The osprey lifts one leg in threat, but the writhing of its prey is of no consequence; the fish collapses and dangles. The osprey gently lowers its leg, turns its head to look about, then lifts its wings, stretching.

In one sudden, graceful motion, it knifes its beak into the fish. This brings on another round of desperate thrashing, the terrible furor of life taking leave. Delicately now, the osprey turns the fish over with one talon, gashes the flesh again, lays the fish back down, and sits erect, watching the horizon. I can see that the osprey has pecked out the eyes; should the osprey drop it, which is unlikely, the blinded fish will be unable to escape. Still, the fish jerks wildly, putting up a determined struggle even as its body is being broken down. I am impressed by the precise, systematic surgery of the osprey's ruthless dismantling.

The osprey leans in, craning head to talons, and begins to pull hard. It twists off the fish's lips. A bright red stream of blood gushes from the side of the fish and streams down the trunk of the tree and pools in the crotch of a branch. The fish thrashes once more, a fierce spasm, and then it is over. The osprey tears off its head.

The bird opens its enormous wings and lifts off the branch. It disappears into the woods, tunneling into an opening in the trees. It will take its meal privately. I think of the poet Mary Oliver, who wrote: "Such beauty as the earth offers must hold great meaning."

Lifting my paddle again, and ignoring the twinge in my neck, I push off against an outcropping of red granite on the island. A breeze is playing across the water; a rogue wind is coming up. I have no idea how long the journey to the beach is; it might be only a mile or two, but it feels like ten. The anticipation of arrival elongates the miles. They are shorter and easier when I'm heading home. I know exactly where I'm headed: to the edge of the sea, that "strange and beautiful place," as Rachel Carson called it, a "marginal world."

It is a place I have returned to again and again over the years, to walk the beaches at all tides, to examine the boulders and eddies and coves along the way, to stir and poke and chase the tiny creatures that populate a continually changing place that is no place, really, more a condition. You cannot say, exactly, where the edge of the sea begins and ends. The tides are sculpted by moons, winds, and storms; they are by turns violent and subtle, yet utterly reliable in the rhythm of their leaving and returning.

When I go to the edge of the sea, I marvel at the constant change, wonder at what has turned up in the swells. More than ever before, this tidal zone draws me with its mystery and movement and magic. I can never sit by the sea; I am always walking alongside it, breathing deeply the fragrant air, rich with ozone and drying seaweed. Strange to think of being grounded by water, but that is exactly what happens to me when I am near the ocean.

The edge of the sea has many voices, as I think of them, some booming, some frantic, some crashing. But the voice I respond most deeply to, listen most closely to, is one that whispers: a susurration of water riffling across clacking stone, mingled with breezes catching in the high grass of the dunes. After years of first finding and then finally hearing and understanding what that voice can teach me, I have just begun to accept the relentless flux that is the condition of my life, of all our lives. Not young, not old; not betrothed, not alone; thinking back, looking forward; not broken, not quite whole anymore, either. But present.

These are my intertidal years.

I reach the sandbar and my kayak crunches into the rocky shore. I know that this beach is often a disappointment to visitors, who complain about the rocks and wonder where the shells are. There are shells, but usually in shards. They are for those who appreciate fragments of poetry, the beauty of which lies as much in a suggestion of what has been lost as in what is preserved; those mysterious, random interruptions and suspended thoughts that invite the reader to imagine the rest, or to marvel at the violent effect of such delicate breaks. Somehow, not having the whole shell makes me more aware of the subtle wash of creamy colors across its surface.

The common purple sea snail makes it to the beach in better shape, perhaps because, improbably, it lives on the surface of the ocean. Its story is sweet and sad. "This snail is remarkable in its adaptation to life as a drifter," I learned from my well-worn Audubon field guide, a book that can achieve the grace of the Psalms. "It manufactures a raft of mucus bubbles to which it clings upside down. If detached from its float, it sinks to the bottom and dies." Difficult to imagine such a fragile hold on life, in a home anchored by no more than the thread of a baby's spittle. But we, too, get turned upside down, and perhaps we only think we have a surer grip; we float our hopes on bubbles of optimism and opportunity, and the lines that keep us alive are easily snipped.

The larger whelks are usually eroded, so what I find on the beach are the thick inner whorls of the shells. Strange that, for us, the shell of a home is a sad or incomplete thing. We describe an early, uninhabitable stage of construction as a shell; a bombed-out shell in wartime; a rotting shell left behind by floods. A shell is an empty place, soulless. And yet, the shell of a sea creature is all the home it has; it is all it needs. I like the idea of fitting perfectly within my shell, and sealing it off against anything that threatens me. In my intertidal years, I finally come to the realization that I no longer want to be around people who make me feel like I am in harm's way. Where once this was thrilling or seductive, appealing in its unending neediness, now it is draining. I'm learning to seal myself off from toxic encounters.

It's hard for most shelled creatures to make any kind of home in this intertidal zone, where they can be swept away on a wave; they're too fragile, too vulnerable to the pounding of surf against stone. That makes the ones that do thrive all the more astonishing: the various mussels, snails, limpets, whelks, rock periwinkles nestled in the ropy weeds. I have to change my focus and come in close to appreciate them; I often take my reading glasses to the beach. It was years before I learned that the rough, chalky surfaces of the boulders at the tide line were actually filled with living creatures; the barnacles were not merely a mineral deposit, as I'd assumed. I've scraped myself against their sharp cones often enough, but I've never been able to pry one off. Waves slide right off their shells, and you need a sharp knife to cut through the strong cement with which they have affixed themselves to their rocks, sealing in life-preserving water during low tides.

Limpets are the most enchanting of these rock dwellers, to my mind, probably because there is something mysterious and poignant about their attachment to home. The limpet is a snail, though its shell isn't whorled; it is a flattened cone, without an opening at the top. The limpets found in my neck of the coast are small, the size of a fingernail, and camouflaged by growths of green marine algae. The limpet will occupy the same spot its entire life. It shapes its shell to match precisely the contour of its rocky perch. After it returns from foraging on the night's high tide, it must find that spot, as it fits nowhere else but on its "home scar," as some poetic scientist called it long ago. I admire the indelibility of that term. The limpet seals itself on its spot so tightly that no brute force can remove it; it will allow itself to be destroyed rather than lose its hold on home.

I think of the limpet when I look back on all the places I've called home, all the houses I thought I would never relinquish, until I had to leave. Each time of moving was difficult, until I somehow fit myself into the new place. I suppose it could be said that I've created home scars in that I've left marks in the very soil and timber of the places I've lived. But from time to time, I find myself envying a creature who will know only one home, with generations of offspring colonizing nearby, a strange, tiny creature for whom there is literally no place like home.

By now I'm hot enough for a swim. Immersion in the cold Atlantic always quiets the throbbing of my mind. In the ocean, my body feels sleeker. The salt water is heavy on my arms, like the satin of a gown. Many people do not like to step into the ocean. The darkness of the water is frightening, and so, too is the thought that you cannot see what you are putting your foot down on. The pull of the powerful, unseen tides and currents is eerie. I love being lifted off my feet; I enjoy the intimacy with the water and the drop into an endless horizon. I once swam for long minutes off the coast of Maine with a seal pup for company and became mesmerized by our dance, by the warmth and humor in the pup's eyes, convinced that I had become a selkie, an enchanted woman-seal at long last returning to her natal element. I realized only too late that what I had become was hypothermic.

I've been swimming every day for the last couple of months, at one with the ancient nymphs who kick and wriggle to safety. There's something primitive about the feeling of washing away pain. Even so, this year I'm aware of how much more careful I have to be about getting in, attuned to half-submerged mossy rocks or sharp eelgrass or rough surf. I used to just run for it. My feet are no longer tolerant of the rough cobbles. It is vexing to consider the onset of frailty, until I consider the alternative: avoid anything dangerous. I am more fearful of the pull of currents and tides than I used to be, but I suspect, and hope, that there will come a time when I am so old that they will not frighten me in the least. I won't mind where they take me; I will be ready to go.

I wade in, shudder with the cold, and then pull for the horizon. I've been relearning my stroke this summer, having decided to take some lessons from a lifeguard. I had always prided myself on staying flat in the water. Wrong.

"We roll, now," the lifeguard told me, shouting a bit, in that infuriating way the young have toward their elders. "You want to maximize your stroke. Reach as far as you can. Your body should never be flat on the water—always on one side or the other. You roll. You reach."

It was annoying to learn to swim all over again. The lifeguard was critical of every move I made: my hand position, my breathing, my head placement.

"Keep your fingers spread. Like a baseball glove."

Here again. The shadows come into play.

"Don't worry," she said. "It will feel awkward at first, but it doesn't look funny. It only feels that way. Everything always feels exaggerated in the water. That's the nature of water."

Quite the philosopher, I think, remembering her instructions as I tunnel through the ocean. The wind is picking up—weather changes so quickly here—and the water is getting choppy. I contract my belly into my backbone and surf the waves, and finally get their syncopation. I feel like I'm climbing a ladder, pulling myself across the swells, rung by rung.

"When you pull through the water, you must reach your arm down low. The water around your body is already moving. You are moving. When you make a shallow stroke, you are only pulling through moving water. You are just pulling through your own motion.

"You must reach deeper. You must reach to where the water is still. Then you will move faster."

Once I'm over being annoyed, I'm amazed at what a swimming lesson has taught me. If I'm a middle-aged dog learning new tricks, I'll be an old dog willing, at least, to be up to my usual tricks. That sounds like a good future to me, no matter how careful I have to be about slipping on rocks.

My reveries are interrupted by the sulfurous smell and the buzzing sound of a gasoline-powered boat. A strong voice cuts across the water.

"Hey, there. You. You swimming. Hey!"

A fisherman is standing in a whaler. The sea is pitching his boat around; he bends to the back to cut off the motor. I look around, dizzy and disoriented. He motions for me to swim in, and cups his hands around his mouth.

"You are too far out!"

I swim in to the far end of the beach, where a rubble of boulders is strewn around, half sunk in sand. I lean on one to catch my breath and clear my ears. The larger ones are encrusted with tiny snails, glued firmly down; the snails at the top of the rocks are already dusted with the salty film left by drying seawater. Their shells are the same pinkish-brown color as the stone and the sand. I stand perfectly still, staring at the boulders glowing rosily in the late afternoon rays of the sun. I wonder if the snails will die desiccated and fall off the rock; I even consider splashing water on them, before I realize how silly that would be. The snails know what they are doing.

Everything seems still and silent. Before I see it, I feel it: there is tremendous movement at my feet. The sand around me is covered with snails, hundreds of them, their fleshy, slimy bodies tipping and pulling out the front, dragging their shells at an impossibly slow pace, leaving behind a glistening, sticky trail. I can see that they are moving only because I am not. By the time a snail has traveled the length of my foot, the shadows have lengthened and the wind has picked up strength as the coral-throated gulls laugh and bark and wheel over the dunes. A crane wings past, making its sharp *click click click* call. I walk the length of the beach back to my boat.

I am always surprised by joy, and that is what is suffusing my entire being. I feel it start deep in my belly and spread up and over my body, and I recognize it for what it is: a slow flush of love for the world—the sheer pleasure of being here, the profound honor of witnessing life. As I paddle home across the pond, I'm overwhelmed with the beauty all around me. There's a lot to enjoy in a life of solitude, I've learned, but I know that I'm not alone, either. Love is all around me.

A splash of white in the distance catches my eye. It is a bride. She seems to be standing at the steps of the porch of a neighbor's house, at the far end of a wide, sloping lawn. She is looking out at the water beyond. All the hope, all the love. All our beginnings, over and over again. The wind gusts, and it is blowing hard. The bride's veil lifts off the stairs and flies behind her like a banner. How brave she is.

I reflexively put my binoculars to my eyes and adjust them to get a better look. The bridesmaids are in black gowns, red shawls wrapped around their shoulders. How clever these children's styles are now; they look like the red-winged blackbirds that careen through the meadow. The groom, with his proud bearing, glances at the musicians, a cellist flanked by a flutist and a violinist. They are pulling their bows across the strings, swaying, bending into the music, but the wind is blowing the sound away from me, and I cannot hear a thing. The wedding is played out in pantomime. Soundlessly, the procession moves down the brick path; soundlessly, the musicians play; soundlessly, the minister says his blessing; soundlessly, the congregation claps and the children cheer a silent kiss.

ACKNOWLEDGMENTS

FIRST A SALUTE, with deepest thanks, to my *House & Garden* colleagues. I am lucky to have worked with such smart, passionate people, who immeasurably enhanced the way I see the world.

Many thanks to Stroller for reading this manuscript with care and concern, and for taking the time to comb through the pages, pointing out distortion and delight alike. Much of the dialogue and all of the events in this book were recorded in journals. Some of it was re-created from memory, which I wouldn't call whole cloth; mine is more cheesecloth.

Great thanks as well to my earliest readers: my sisters, Nicole Browning and Michele O'Rourke; my brother, Philippe Browning; and my sister-in-law Diane McDaniel, an excellent editor by profession and inclination. Sarah Finne Robinson and Caroline Cunningham Young provided copious notes. Peter Buckley was wise and patient; Lyris Schonholz was eagle-eyed. Cynthia Frank, Abigail Congdon, Frances Palmer, Fen Montaigne, Kay Calvert, Jim Manzi, David Rawle, and Kathryn Welsh Grantham gave me suggestions, recipes, playlists, and delicious dinners; Laurie Hays helped me cook up the title. Thanks as well to Dan Bucsescu, who designed my new house, and Rick Messier and his team, who so beautifully built it. Thanks to Sue

Mandel and Cynthia Hampton of the Environmental Defense Fund for including me in the conversation about the world's biggest problem. Jacqueline Novogratz inspired me to find the RESTART button.

My editor, the indefatigable Lauren LeBlanc, guided me with sensitive and engaging questions. She has what we all want: wisdom beyond her years. My publisher, James Atlas, approached me out of the blue—I hadn't seen him in years—with a book idea about what it was like to lose my job, and I was able to tell him that I had just spent the last year writing such a thing. Kismet. While most publishers think the sky is falling and are running for cover, Jim has created a new book company, and I'm honored to be included in his radical endeavor.

Byron Dobell was one of the first people I worked for after I graduated from college, and he has remained a dear friend and an honest critic; thank you to him and to his wife, Alex Birnbaum, for their help.

Amanda Urban was also an early boss, and I tell the story of my relationship with her to young people starting out as an example of You Never Know . . . Binky hired me at *Esquire* in the late '70s. I was reporting to at least ten men, who had wildly (and shocking—I was so naïve!) different ideas about what a secretary was supposed to do. Suffice it to say that after she found me in the bathroom, crying out of sheer frustration, a secretary who had been at the magazine for decades showed me the desk drawer in which she kept a bottle of bourbon and a loaded gun. Binky was an exacting boss who brooked no nonsense, and I was the kind of college grad who thought I was too good for the job. She set me straight. After she left the magazine to become a literary agent, I didn't see her for years. Then I bumped into her at a restaurant. She remarked on how much she liked my column in *House & Garden*, and she urged me to write a book. The next time I saw her she demanded my manuscript. I was still so afraid of her that I got to work. You never know who will turn your life around; Binky opened up a new world.

To all, thanks for the love that grows slowly. It is the most profound.